BRAM STOKER'S *DRACULA*

Continuum *Reader's Guides*

Continuum *Reader's Guides* are clear, concise and accessible introductions to classic literary texts. Each book explores the themes, context, criticism and influence of key works, providing a practical introduction to close reading and guiding the reader towards a thorough understanding of the text. Ideal for undergraduate students, the guides provide an essential resource for anyone who needs to get to grips with a literary text.

Achebe's *Things Fall Apart* – Ode Ogede
Austen's *Emma* – Gregg A. Hecimovich
Chaucer's *The Canterbury Tales* – Gail Ashton
Conrad's *Heart of Darkness* – Allan Simmons
Dickens's *Great Expectations* – Ian Brinton
Eliot's *Middlemarch* – Josie Billington
Fitzgerald's *The Great Gatsby* – Nicolas Tredell
Fowles's *The French Lieutenant's Woman* – William Stephenson
Salinger's *The Catcher in the Rye* – Sarah Graham
William Blake's *Poetry* – Jonathan Roberts

BRAM STOKER'S *DRACULA*
A READER'S GUIDE

WILLIAM HUGHES

continuum

Continuum International Publishing Group
The Tower Building   80 Maiden Lane
11 York Road   Suite 704
London SE1 7NX   New York, NY 10038

www.continuumbooks.com

© William Hughes 2009

British Library Cataloguing-in-Publication Data
A catalogue record for this book is available from the British Library.

ISBN: 978-0-8264-9536-5 (hardback)
      978-0-8264-9537-2 (paperback)

Library of Congress Cataloging-in-Publication Data
A catalog record for this book is available from the Library of Congress.

Typeset by Newgen Imaging Systems Pvt Ltd, Chennai, India
Printed and bound in Great Britain by MPG Books Ltd,
Bodmin, Cornwall

CONTENTS

ACKNOWLEDGEMENTS

Many friends and colleagues have supported me in my work during the two years it has taken me to complete this book. Of these, I would like to thank, in particular, Andrew Smith (University of Glamorgan); Sue Zlosnik (Manchester Metropolitan University); Ben Fisher (University of Mississippi); Tracey Hill (Bath Spa University); Caroline Netherton (Bath Spa University); Ardel Thomas (San Francisco Community College); Jacques Sirgent (Musée des Vampires, Les Lilas); Lana Maht Wiggins (University of New Orleans); Stephen Gregg (Bath Spa University); Ellen McWilliams (Bath Spa University); Morgaine Merch Lleuad (Bath Spa University); and Nick Drew (Bath Spa University). I would also like to thank Anna Sandeman and Colleen Coalter at Continuum Books, for their patience and support.

I would also like to acknowledge the consistent support and friendship of Peggy and the late Bill Burns; Carol Killey and Brian Killey, jr; Margaret and Gary Fagan; Ina de Souza and Martin Houghton; May Wallace; John Cadby and Harry Cadby; Bill Beaven; Don Farmer; Sid Hall; Mike Keveren and Sylvia Girard-Keveren; and my old friends from Penrhyn Street, Julie Maylor and Guy Williams.

This book is dedicated, with love, to someone who changed my life for the better:

Cyflwynir y llyfr hwn, gyda chariad, i Gillian Wheeler

William Hughes
Llangollen, 25 August 2008

AUTHOR'S NOTE

All references to *Dracula* are taken from Bram Stoker, *Dracula*, edited by William Hughes and Diane Mason (Bath: Artswork Books, 2007). Page references are given in parentheses throughout the text of this Guide.

CHAPTER 1

CONTEXTS

STOKER'S LIFE

Abraham Stoker junior was born on 8 November 1847, the third child of a Protestant family resident in the north Dublin suburb of Clontarf. He was, by his own admission, a sickly child whose 'long illness' found him 'often at the point of death'.[1] The exact nature of this illness has never been satisfactorily defined. Biographical and critical speculations have configured it as a fever, possibly associated with the Irish Famine of 1846, with childhood asthma, or with psychological trauma.[2] Whatever its cause, the illness confined him first to bed, and subsequently to the family home, where he was kept amused by his mother's recollections of the Sligo cholera epidemic of 1832 and her recounting of traditional Irish tales of ghosts and fairies.

Presumably because of his illness, Stoker was educated first at home and later at Bective House, a private Anglican day-school in Dublin. His school education and middle-class origins facilitated his entry to Trinity College, the sole constituent College of the University of Dublin, on 2 November 1864, at the age of 16. Stoker was not a gifted scholar. Despite his claim that he 'had got Honours in Pure Mathematics' – a statement frequently accepted without question by biographers and critics alike – Stoker's graduation as an ordinary Bachelor in Arts on 1 March 1870 was undistinguished by any formal Honours. His Master's degree, which was awarded on 9 February 1875, was nothing more than an honorary addition to his undergraduate title, being awarded without the need for further study.[3]

Stoker did make a reputation, however, as a university athlete and all-round college personality. He played rugby football for the

University between 1867 and 1871, and was awarded silver cups for athletics and weightlifting.[4] He was equally prominent in the debating chamber: in 1869 and 1872, respectively, Stoker was elected President of the University's Philosophical Society and Auditor of the rival Historical Society, and he remains the only individual to had led both groups. Student debating societies such as these brought gifted undergraduates into the company of the academic, religious and political worthies of their day. Stoker's debating-room contemporaries included the undergraduates Oscar Wilde and his brother Willie, as well as Edward Carson, who was later to act for the Marquis of Queensberry at Oscar's trial for libel. Stoker was associated, also, with Oscar's father, the ophthalmic specialist and amateur Egyptologist Sir William Wilde, with Edward Dowden, Professor of English Literature at Dublin University, and with the painter John Butler Yeats.

Stoker joined the Irish Civil Service in 1866 while he was still technically a student at the University.[5] While researching his first book, *The Duties of Clerks of Petty Sessions in Ireland* (1879), he began to develop his writing style as a novelist and essayist. He wrote theatrical reviews for the *Dublin Mail* from 1871, and was, for four months in 1873, the editor of a daily newspaper, *The Irish Echo*. Though his first short story, 'The Crystal Cup' (1872), was printed in *London Society*, a minor English periodical, Stoker published the majority of his earliest works – all serial novellas – in a Dublin penny journal, *The Shamrock*, in 1875. Critics have often depicted these works as precursors to *Dracula*: their incidents and characterizations, however, are inclined more to the moralistic and the adventurous rather than to the generically Gothic.[6] Stoker was notably unsuccessful in placing work with more prestigious English journals, and had fiction returned by *The Cornhill Magazine*, *Macmillan's Magazine*, *Temple Bar* and *Blackwood's*.[7]

It was through his work as an unpaid theatrical critic that Stoker met the charismatic English actor, Henry Irving (1838–1905). He consistently praised Irving's style of acting in the *Dublin Mail* and dined with him on several occasions. Stoker regarded the friendship between the two in almost spiritual terms, frequently betraying an intensity of emotional commitment which Irving's son came to despise as 'sentimental idolatry'.[8] Whatever the case, Stoker was persuaded, against the advice offered by his father, to resign his civil service post towards the close of 1878 in order to take up Irving's offer of employment as Acting Manager of the Lyceum Theatre, London. Impulsively, Stoker brought forward the date of his marriage to Florence Balcombe, a former sweetheart of Oscar Wilde, and the newly-weds took lodgings near the theatre before moving to fashionable Cheyne Walk in Chelsea, where the pre-Raphaelite painter Dante Gabriel Rossetti was a near neighbour.

Stoker was to retain his position under Irving – which made him effectively the actor's accountant, secretary, ghost-writer and public spokesman – for 27 years. He was, though, still active as a writer, and, in addition to dramatic journalism and travel writing, produced *Under the Sunset*, a collection of macabre short stories for children, in 1882. His first novel, *The Snake's Pass* (1890) was a romantic work which set the tone for much of Stoker's subsequent output. Romance and adventure writing, in varying proportions, influence all of Stoker's novels. The supernatural, real or imagined, is only prominent in works written after *Dracula* (1897), most notably *The Mystery of the Sea* (1902), *The Jewel of Seven Stars* (1903), the *faux* vampire novel, *The Lady of the Shroud* (1909) and Stoker's final novel, *The Lair of the White Worm* (1911). Prior to Irving's death in 1905, Stoker's fiction was written on a part-time basis, often while on holiday or when touring with the Lyceum company.

The demands of his theatrical post undoubtedly strained Stoker's marriage. The long working days of the London theatrical season preceded months spent on tour in the English regions and the United States. Irving's lavish entertaining, to which Florence was occasionally invited, did bring the Stokers into contact with literary lions, political grandees and theatrical personalities: among his many associates he numbered the Poet Laureate, Alfred, Lord Tennyson, the Liberal statesman, W. E. Gladstone, the explorer, Sir Richard Burton, and Sir Arthur Conan Doyle, creator of Sherlock Holmes. It was Stoker who organized the return of Irving's body to London, after the actor died on tour in 1905, and these final exertions on his employer's behalf precipitated his own decline into ill health. Stoker suffered a paralytic stroke soon after Irving's interment, and found both his eyesight and his movement impaired. Notably, Stoker's only son, baptized Irving Noel Thornley, dropped his Godfather's name in adulthood, and apparently believed that the demanding actor had 'worn Bram out'.[9]

The six years between the deaths of the two associates are remarkable not only for the three novels which Stoker produced but also for the variety of literary tasks he undertook in order to maintain his household. Stoker became a prolific writer of short fiction, published in popular journals and the collection *Snowbound* (1908), and produced a eulogistic biography, *Personal Reminiscences of Henry Irving* (1906). He also published essays on dramatic and literary topics, conducted a series of interviews with former Lyceum associates in *The Daily Chronicle*, and produced an idiosyncratic study of imposture, *Famous Impostors* (1910). These projects appear to have brought him comparatively little financial reward. Stoker supplemented his royalties by becoming business manager to a short-lived West End musical, undertook a lecture tour in the English provinces and organized the British section of the 1908 Paris Theatrical Exhibition.

By 1911, Stoker faced a severe financial crisis. He was bedridden and weak, suffered from Bright's Disease, a kidney disorder, and – according to one biographer – may also have contracted syphilis.[10] Stoker died at his home in Pimlico, London, on 20 April 1912: his death certificate emphasized 'exhaustion' as a likely cause of death.[11] He was cremated following a short service at Golders Green, London, attended by the novelists Hall Caine and Ford Madox Hueffer, the actress Geneviève Ward, and Laurence Irving, the actor's second son. Despite the newspaper obituaries which sought to claim him for the theatre, it may be pertinent to note that Stoker's death certificate described him as holding the 'rank or profession' of 'author'.[12]

MASCULINITY, FEMININITY AND SEXUAL IDENTITY

Recent criticism has contended that the Stoker family's bourgeois origins did not qualify them as outright members of the ruling Anglo-Irish ascendancy. They were, by all accounts, representatives of a middle-class professional meritocracy rather than an hereditary aristocracy, an aspiring class whose codes of manners and taste were dependent upon the precedents established by the Protestant ascendancy.[13] It is likely that Stoker's education, chosen by his civil-servant father, would have schooled him in the discourses and social graces which linked the Anglicized Anglo-Irish gentleman to his English counterpart – temperate Protestantism, modern chivalry and a vision of masculinity premised as much upon athleticism as it was upon manners.

Stoker, in his biography of Irving, depicted himself as 'that aim of a university education *mens sana in corpore sano*'.[14] The ideal of 'a healthy mind in a healthy body' is central to the emphatic masculinity exemplified in both the author's public persona and his fiction. The single-sex environments of public school, College, gentlemen's clubs and the professions foster a culture where shared values of trust between men, and chivalric deference to women, are viewed as defining factors.[15] These specific values are consistently referenced throughout Stoker's fiction and journalism. They are present in *Dracula*, but demonstrated most emphatically in *The Mystery of the Sea* (1902), where gentlemanly trust, marshalled in the defence of an abducted heroine, demonstrably overcomes the pressures exerted by self-interest, religious sectarianism and national identity. In the context of Stoker's fiction, a healthy mind is as much a matter of moral and behavioural regularity as it is one of intellectual attainment.

The moral purity of male community is potentially suspect, however, simply because its gendered identity excludes women. If the homosocial is acceptable, even laudable, in Victorian culture, the homosexual and the effeminate are not – as Wilde was to discover at Oxford.[16] Stoker's hearty public behaviour conceals a more ambiguous introspection upon male community revealed only through correspondence unpublished in his lifetime. Stoker was well known within Dublin University as an apologist for the then-controversial verse of the American poet, Walt Whitman.[17] Though his public focus was the apparent misinterpretation of Whitman's attitude towards women, Stoker's private correspondence with the poet investigates the relationship that might develop between an older and a younger man. Indeed, its tone hovers uneasily between adolescent adulation and a more ambiguous, if not inviting, homo-eroticism – most notably when he thanks the poet 'for all the love and sympathy you have given me in common with my kind'.[18] Whatever Stoker's intentions in writing to Whitman in this manner, this private letter, one of several, has fuelled speculations regarding the author's sexuality. At the very least it is evidence, alongside Stoker's relationships with Dowden and Irving, of what Maurice Richardson called 'an unusually strong father fixation' and the author's status as 'a born hero-worshipper'. At most, its closing sentence might be deployed in order to configure Stoker as a closet homosexual – a possibility which Talia Schaffer explores in a reading of both *Dracula* and Stoker's behaviour following the fall of Oscar Wilde.[19] Stoker's personal sexual orientation – and, indeed, its alleged influence upon *Dracula* and his other writings – still remains, however, a matter of speculation rather than of certainty.

If the fictional heroes of Stoker's fiction embody a conservative and heterosexual perception of physical and moral manliness, then their female counterparts project a more ambiguous alternation between active and passive femininity. Despite his distaste for the feminist leanings of the so-called New Woman – a figure mentioned twice in *Dracula* (133) and depicted by implication in Stoker's 1906 novel, *The Man* – the author's heroines are often resourceful figures. Their resourcefulness, though, is characteristically deployed in the service of the chivalric males with whom they are associated: they do not strive to enter the professions, to gain sexual freedom or to affect the bluff frankness of male conversation. That said, they are capable of moments of physical bravery and endurance: Betty Pole in *Miss Betty* (1898) challenges a highwayman, while Teuta in *The Lady of the Shroud* takes up a sword. Even Mina Harker in *Dracula* endures cold weather and resists predatory vampires, though her emphasized skills of organization, shorthand and typing are perhaps most useful to her male associates.

Assertive women appear to be fascinating, if not to Stoker himself then at least to his readership. They are, though, safely contained in fiction in a way that they cannot easily be within a culture fearful of the moral and social changes they may bring. The compromise characteristic of Stoker's fiction is to bring the assertive heroine back into a conventional patriarchal relationship, usually by having the hero first rescue and then marry her. This is as true of Mina as it is of Teuta, and of Marjory Anita Drake in *The Mystery of the Sea*: even Lucy Westenra may be comprehended by this pattern within Stoker's fiction, given the symbolism that links her final death to a symbolic representation, alternately, of marriage or of marital sexual initiation (259–61). Stoker is thus both a participant in the late-nineteenth-century debate upon gender and an idealist who looks backwards to a period when the gap between the sexes was more clearly and consistently signalled. If anything, his works insist upon the unchanging nature of masculine chivalry, and its central concern with protecting the female, as a way of disarming the threat posed by the perceptibly unstable sexual boundaries associated with the close of the nineteenth century.

RACE, NATION AND DEGENERATION

The related issues of male effeminacy and female assertiveness were central to a broader fin-de-siècle debate upon cultural and racial degeneration. The Victorian fin de siècle (literally, 'the end of the century') was approached with a combination of dread and celebration comparable to that associated with the Millennium of 1999–2000. The confident public celebration of achievements in culture and technology was paralleled by a fearful sense that the morals, art and even physique of the nation had entered into a degenerative decline often referred to as 'decadence'. For those preoccupied with the contemplation of cultural decline, the realization that some citizens might consciously identify with the decadence brought further misgivings: the enemies of progress and of the nation might be found within as well as beyond national borders.

Stoker, in many respects, was informally aligned with this latter preoccupation. His journalism betrays an intolerance of vagrants and negroes, just as his fiction exhibits a distaste for the urban working classes and the immigrant peoples who increasingly lived among them at the close of the century.[20] He appears to have been well read in the polemical and scientific literature of the period, and references the work of the Italian criminal psychologist Cesare Lombroso in *Dracula* not merely by name (385), but also implicitly in the detail of Harker's depiction of the Count at the novel's opening (58–9).[21] The Count is, as Mina notes, 'a criminal and of criminal type' (385): his ability to change the lives and identities of those whom he encounters recalls how crime becomes, at the fin de siècle, as much a medical problem as a moral issue.

The rhetorical association of degeneration with infection was further reinforced by the rise of a racist as well as criminological science of eugenics. If an individual's criminal tendency was a result of bad breeding, then certain racial groups were equally condemned through their perceived inferiority or hereditary criminality. Stoker, notoriously, gave his degenerate Count a 'beaky nose' (215) and a tendency to hoard money (88), and thus aligned him to the stereotypical Jewish moneylender, an unscrupulous financial vampire.[22] Explicitly Jewish characters elsewhere in Stoker's fiction receive as little sympathy as Immanuel Hildesheim, the Count's agent at Galatz, who has 'a nose like a sheep' (392). Though trading within Britain, they are generally depicted as being superficially domesticated, their avarice betraying a concealed foreignness that has subtly infiltrated British society.[23]

The fin de siècle was, further, a period of mass (though not exclusively Jewish) immigration from eastern Europe: much of the polemic of the period addressed the integration of immigrant peoples into the urban working-class population, and in particular the sexual corruption of gentile womanhood.[24] *Dracula* may draw upon this cultural prejudice, though it may also have a specific literary source in *Trilby* (1894), a novel written by the *Punch* cartoonist George Du Maurier, and produced as a London stage play by Beerbohm Tree in 1895. The sexual predation of Du Maurier's eastern European Jewish villain, Svengali, is facilitated in *Trilby* by his use of hypnotism – a technique which Count Dracula himself employs in his exploitation of Mina.[25] Criticism, additionally, has identified the Count with a broader notion of invasion from the orient, a 'reverse colonization' that undermines the expansion and aggrandizement associated with Empire.[26] Stoker, notably, emphasizes the almost foreign dialect of the thirsty working classes who enter the Count's employment as unthinkingly as the Szgany the vampire employs in Transylvania. It is the dialect-speaking children of the London proletariat who fall so easily victim to the Count's first English conquest, Lucy Westenra (220–1). National integrity – in manners as much as in bodies – is a fragile thing, and at its most brittle when embodied in both a brutish proletariat, and in vulnerable women and children. Seemingly, it is only an Anglo-European alliance of gentlemanly Britons, a modern American adventurer and a patriarchal Teutonic Dutchman, that may effectively counter the incursion of the Feudal, backward-looking East represented by the Count and his minions.[27] *Dracula*, in this respect, recalls the sentiments of Stoker's early travel narrative, *A Glimpse of America* (1886), in its assertion of 'the instinct of a common race' which, by definition, excludes all others from acceptance into brotherhood.[28]

Dracula, as these readings suggest, might well be regarded as the most fearful narrative of the fin de siècle, a dire warning of the impending collapse of the known world. This is certainly the view frequently taken by modern criticism, though it is worth noting that Stoker's contemporaries regarded the novel as little more than a piece of popular fiction, with no subtle or prophetic content.[29] Bearing this in mind, it would be easy to dismiss modern interpretations of *Dracula* as little more than anachronistic impositions upon what is nothing more than popular entertainment. It is in the popular, though, away from the restrictions of high culture and the censure of elite taste, that the greatest freedom to express dis-ease or to openly celebrate crude power is to be found. Stoker's novel, undoubtedly, is a product of its age, and an index to the languages and the issues that mobilized its fears and its aspirations. Whether or not the author consciously deployed these things is irrelevant: what matters is the novel's accepted status as a work that facilitates an interface between a well-documented historical and cultural period and an author increasingly subjected to reliable biography. Despite the enduring prejudice that still seems to accompany any work deemed popular, *Dracula* is now, without question, one of the central texts of modern literary criticism.

CHAPTER 2

LANGUAGE, STYLE AND FORM

DRACULA AS A GOTHIC NOVEL

Modern academic criticism, as Glennis Byron suggests, regularly associates *Dracula* with a single literary genre, the Gothic.[1] Byron's assessment echoes the opinions of a number – though by no means a majority – of the novel's contemporary reviewers, who readily compared *Dracula* to Gothic writings by, among others, Edgar Allan Poe, J. S. Le Fanu and Ann Radcliffe.[2] The choice of authors named in these late-Victorian reviews is telling. No distinction was seemingly drawn in 1897 between the 'now almost forgotten romances' of Ann Radcliffe, published at the close of the eighteenth century, nominally Victorian works such as 'The Fall of the House of Usher' (1839) and *Wuthering Heights* (1847), and comparatively recent vampire narratives such as J. S. Le Fanu's 'Carmilla' (1871–2).[3] Modern criticism is more delicate with these distinctions, however, and has come to subdivide the Gothic into a succession of phases or tendencies, variously divided by content, narrative style and the power relationships which they depict.[4]

The Gothic novel traces its ancestry back to *The Castle of Otranto* (1764) by Horace Walpole, a short work which established a matrix out of which other, more substantial, narratives might be generated. In its depiction of vengeful ghosts and feudal tyranny, Walpole's novel countered the rationalism of the then ascendant Enlightenment. Beyond its assertion of a powerful supernatural, *The Castle of Otranto* was instrumental in popularizing a further range of themes and devices whose presence punctuates the genre from the eighteenth century to the present. These include the themes of imprisonment, incest and of the misappropriation of property, particularly through marriage or murder. Also established in the earliest days of the Gothic was the figure of the Gothic Hero, a villainous anti-hero gifted, if not with superhuman or supernatural strength or longevity, then at least with a greater capacity for both evil and suffering. This figure, in the form of rapacious monks and grasping guardians, is associated in particular with another recurrent Gothic theme, that of the imperilled woman. Her status as a chattel lightly given in marriage, as an heiress to be possessed, sexually or legally, along with her property, or as a potential victim of male violence, is central not merely to Walpole's novel but also to the late-eighteenth-century works of Ann Radcliffe, disparagingly cited by Stoker's anonymous 1897 reviewer.

The relative decline of Gothic in the first three decades of the nineteenth century almost certainly prompted the progressive development of the genre away from the medieval and Continental settings favoured in the eighteenth century, and motivated a corresponding shift to modern manners and recognizably British settings. Established sites of Gothic peril, such as the castle, the Inquisition and the convent, were replaced by the contemporary country house, the city streets, the lunatic asylum and the laboratory, as the genre came to embody and explore the perceived threats posed by a secular century. The eighteenth-century distaste for, and suspicion of, Roman Catholicism was similarly eclipsed as other perceived enemies of liberty and nation arose to challenge the stability of British modernity. Priests, monks and nuns, the stock figures of eighteenth-century Gothic, were replaced, significantly, not merely by obviously alien figures such as the immigrant or the Jew but also deviant members of otherwise authoritative and thoroughly recognizable professions – the mad doctor, the unethical vivisectionist, the scheming lawyer. The Gothic, as it were, had entered the very fabric of domestic and secular identity.

As the presence of these latter figures might suggest, one of the most significant developments within Victorian Gothic was the collapse of hitherto clear-cut distinctions between such conventional opposites as self and Other, good and evil, domestic and foreign. *Dracula*, with its range of transitional identities and conditions – the novelistic hesitations, for example, between life/death, science/spirituality or even fiancée/bride – is thus a versatile text through which fin-de-siècle challenges to certainty and integrity might be explored. In a sense, the novel's depiction of bodies and souls in a state of flux between known and unprecedented conditions facilitates the juxtaposition of the familiar and the unfamiliar: through a form of doubling, it allows the character to either perceive, or to be perceived through, its own deviance from a familiar norm. Jonathan Harker is a case in point. His status as a bourgeois parvenu – he has qualified as a solicitor while working as a provincial clerk (55) rather than by way of attending the London Inns of Court – is progressively undermined as he moves further east on his way to join Count Dracula. On this journey into the unknown, Harker is forced to rely not on his mastery of conventional English but upon an imperfect command of German (41) and the translations from Slovakian and Serbian dialects contained in his 'polyglot dictionary' (46). Other indicators of regularity are lost as his journey progresses: his destination is not to be found on any map (42); the letter, or word of mouth, replaces the telegram (44); the diligence (44) or calèche (51) takes the place of the train which, in any case, is perceived as unpunctual by English standards (43). Harker progressively loses control of both his environment and his capacity to effectively communicate both his observations and state of mind: his final collapse into a condition corresponding to a nervous breakdown is motivated by both Harker's incomprehension at seeing his host descend, *face down*, the vertiginous castle walls (75), and by the impossibility of the Count growing visibly younger almost before his eyes (92). Harker is a man obsessed with detail, a rationalist and an empiricist who deals in facts; yet the accumulation of data overwhelms him, pointing him towards the impossible truth that his world-view is incapable of comprehending adequately the situation he has placed himself in. Captivity further exacerbates Harker's self-conscious secondary status as a man of humble origins, acting not for himself but as an agent for others. He is never 'his own man'. Clare Simmons rightly argues that Harker's helplessness effectively feminizes him, so that he accedes, in her reading, to the 'masculine' prerogatives of the Count.[5] One might consider also that he becomes subject, at the same time, to the pre-modern feudal mentality that distinguishes the backward East from the progressive West.

In this respect, *Dracula* might well be regarded as a novel which revivifies the conventions of the Female Gothic, usually associated in criticism with fiction cast in the mould of Ann Radcliffe. The Female Gothic, in the late twentieth and early twenty-first centuries, has come to exceed its original critical definition in Ellen Moers' *Literary Women* (1963), where it was associated with works produced by women writers, with fear and, specifically, with the traumas of pregnancy, childbirth and parenthood.[6] Its association now is with scenarios of female peril through abduction or imprisonment, with narratives of sexual danger, and with the threat of change that the latter may bring both to the physiological self and to its cultural value. The disdainful Count Dracula, as Fred Botting argues, is a lineal descendent of Radcliffe's imperious and saturnine Montoni in *The Mysteries of Udolpho* (1795).[7] If one may discern a relatively conventional example of the Female Gothic in the effective abduction by the vampire of, in succession, Lucy's soul (250) and Mina's consciousness (370), then one may perceive, in addition, a further development in the novel's feminization of Harker. There is, of course, a further suggestion of homo-eroticism: as Christopher Craft notes, 'the sexual threat that this novel first evokes, manipulates, sustains, but never finally represents is that Dracula will seduce, penetrate, drain another male'.[8] The Count's 'threat', though, is associated with power as much as with sexuality. Though male, Harker is owned, dispossessed, disposed of, just like a Radcliffean heroine. It is only through courage and struggle, initially realized in his own descent down the castle wall, he effectively rescues (and, indeed, redeems) himself. If his subject position unmans him, then his endeavour regenerates his manliness, and reorientates him squarely within gendered Western power relations. Contemplating his immediate faith before descending for the first time, he states: 'At the worst it can only be death; and a man's death is not a calf's' (87).

Though the Count may well be considered a lineal descendent of the eighteenth-century anti-hero, he is equally one-half of another persistent Gothic convention – the double or doppelgänger. *Dracula* is punctuated by doublings: East and West, modern and feudal, technology and religion, are just three of the binaries whose juxtaposition advances the plot. In his own right, though, the nineteenth-century Count constitutes a double not merely of the exceptional mortal he was prior to his vampirism (284), but also of his contemporary nemesis, Van Helsing. Though vampire and vampire hunter have long been considered to be structurally intimate, Victor Sage was the first critic to associate this doubling with Stoker's interest in Lombroso's scientific criminology. Recalling Harker's description of the Count's markedly 'aquiline' face with its 'bushy' eyebrows 'almost meeting over the nose' (58), Sage correctly identifies that Stoker 'makes a point of giving Van Helsing, the wise Magus from Eastern Europe, these symptoms of degeneracy'. This apparently paradoxical doubling is revealed to be logical when it is noted that Lombroso specifically considered genius a variety of insanity, and thus a type of degeneration.[9] This clarifies Seward's contention, after his first entry to Lucy's tomb, that Van Helsing, being 'abnormally clever' (247) might also be mad. The doubling between the two is thus more complex than a mere opposition: it is a difference of degree, with one form of deviance (forward-looking genius) being more tolerated than the other (degeneration, an atavistic resemblance to one's savage ancestors). Andrew Smith is therefore quite correct when he argues that 'Van Helsing, a doctor of medicine, philosophy and the law, can be read as a highly professionalised version of the Count': quite simply, the vampire's most dreadful quality is his assimilation of the modern, his slow but sure advance into integration with the contemporary world.[10] The Count's library, which includes books relating to English 'history, geography, politics, political economy, botany, geology, law' (60), represents but the amateur equivalent of the professional works through which the novel's professionals have been educated. Where both the hero and the villain are deviant, the outcome of their conflict can never be straightforward. *Dracula*, in this respect, represents a departure from the somewhat conventional morality displayed by most Gothic texts.

NARRATIVE STYLE

Dracula is a novel driven by documentation. It is advanced through diaries, personal and business letters, witness statements, medical diagnoses, newspaper journalism and telegrams. The value of these supposedly authoritative eyewitness accounts is in no sense stable or assured, however, despite a prefatory promise that 'all the records chosen' are 'given from the standpoints and within the range of knowledge of those who made them' (40). Original testimony is scarce in *Dracula*, even the account presented to the reader being explicitly a copy of a copy (268), typed by Mina in order to synthesize and integrate the disparate material provided by many fictional participants. A process of editing, of ordering, even of translation, has taken place. This often scarce-acknowledged process in itself recalls the framing devices of early Gothic, from the fictional translator of *The Castle of Otranto*, through to the Italian gentleman who hands to the English traveller the written confession which becomes the central narrative of Ann Radcliffe's *The Italian* (1797). It is a framing device which persists in contemporary Gothic, as is testified, for example, by the title and organization of Anne Rice's *Interview with the Vampire* (1976).

Though it does not explicitly call itself such, *Dracula* is structurally a case, and is cast very much in the mould of Robert Louis Stevenson's *The Strange Case of Dr Jekyll and Mr Hyde* (1886). Significantly, therefore, all 'the records chosen' relate to the outcome of the case, and strive to *prove* 'a history almost at variance with the possibilities of later-day belief' (40) as well as to justify the extreme measures through which the case was pursued and concluded. Stevenson's *Strange Case*, however, was not the literary precedent most frequently adopted by Stoker's reviewers in order to explain the structure of *Dracula* to their fin-de-siècle readership. Despite the scientific and Gothic associations of Jekyll's physical and moral degeneration into Hyde, reviewers referred any reader seeking a literary comparison to the slightly earlier writings of Wilkie Collins, author of *The Woman in White* (1860) and *The Moonstone* (1868).[11]

Collins, though usually identified with the Sensation Novel, a genre which fictionalized scandals and secrets in high society, is an obvious choice. His novel-length work, though seldom directly concerned with ghosts, often displays characteristically Gothic motifs: *The Woman in White*, for example, revolves around the doubling of two half-sisters and the machinations of a foreign anti-hero, the Italian nobleman Count Fosco. That novel, similarly, features a somewhat inept bourgeois hero, Walter Hartright who, nevertheless attains a form of assertive masculinity, comparable to that gained by Jonathan Harker in *Dracula*, through mental and physical struggle and his unflinching determination to release the heroine from unjustified imprisonment and false identity.[12]

The anonymous reviewer for the *St James' Gazette* suggests that the documentary style of *Dracula* 'makes [Stoker's] imaginative impossibilities appear not only possible but convincing' quite simply because the author 'has followed the method of Wilkie Collins, couching his tale in the form of diary and letter, and adding evidence to evidence with every circumstance of invoice, telegram, and legal document'.[13] Collins, like Stoker, qualified as a barrister but never practised law: the two novelists do not appear to have been acquaintances, though they shared a common friend in the author Hall Caine who, as 'Hommy Beg', was the dedicatee of *Dracula*. Stoker was almost certainly familiar with Collins's fiction, and no doubt with the dramatization of his works upon the London stage. The difference between *Dracula* and *The Woman in White* is less a degree of style and more a matter of stated purposefulness. Though Collins reassures the reader that 'the story here presented will be told by more than one pen, as the story of an offence against the laws is told in court by more than one witness', the narrative is emphatic that 'the Law is still, in certain inevitable cases, the pre-engaged servant of the long purse'.[14] Legal corruption certainly does feature in *Dracula*: Arthur Holmwood uses his title to deflect a policeman's attention from an act of housebreaking (336–7, 343), and Harker, a solicitor, suggests that 'Judge Moneybag' (377), or bribery, will bring about a desired (though not strictly legal) outcome. If formal law is corrupted or subverted in *Dracula*, though, it is because the ends are made to justify the means within the novel. Effectively, a revised morality and an alternative pattern of legal ethics are projected upon the characters in response to the legally unprecedented problem of vampirism. The law, with its materialistic concerns for property and ownership, paradoxically protects the vampire and by implication assists his colonization of London. The Count, though wealthy, does not even have to deploy a 'long purse' in order to gain the protection of the law – his wealth in England buys him property, privacy and assistance through conventional methods of contracts, mortgages and wages rather than by bribery. British law thus protects the Count fully and, reciprocally, would prototypically react in a punitive manner towards those, such as Van Helsing, who would possess themselves of the Count's property or do injury to his person.

It is the chivalric defence of the female that most facilitates the novel's undoing of the deference conventionally given by the citizen to statute law. Lucy and Mina are left relatively unprotected by the criminal and civil codes that protect the Count. The inflexibility of statute law is therefore compensated for by the consistent and chivalric behaviour of the male devoted to the service of the female: the unwritten law that is held as a common link between like-minded and selfless individuals is thus proclaimed as an essential, true and flexible response capable of guiding the self in unprecedented circumstances. Conveniently, too, because the threatened women of *Dracula* are capable of being associated with racial and national identity, and with spirituality, the defence of the fictional individual becomes implicitly an act that touches upon the whole unknowing though embattled British nation. Westenra, the surname of the Count's first English female victim has, in this context, an undoubtedly symbolic resonance. Lucy is, literally, the 'light of the west', and if on one level her suitors seek to preserve her from 'paths of flame' (250) and an eternity in hell, then they seek also to save her from the odious embraces of a predatory foreign invader.[15] Lucy is, in a sense, a synecdoche – a part which may stand for a whole – in that her fate may credibly be the fate of every decent English woman, should the Count's campaign succeed. She is the smallest, and thus by definition, the most vulnerable component of her sex, her race and her nation. If the law of words, precedents and statutes is too inflexible to protect her, then an another, founded upon standards that are consistent though not necessarily written, must arise to protect her and her fellows. Van Helsing, who is explicitly qualified 'a lawyer as well as a doctor' (206), and whose knowledge embraces both science and spirituality, is the catalyst that facilitates the novel's ethical, as well as epistemological, revisionism.

Van Helsing's formal qualifications are echoed in the interdisciplinary activities of his pupil, Seward, who is not merely a 'mad doctor' or asylum-keeper but who also acts a medico-jurist (288) – a physician qualified to give evidence in criminal cases where a plea of insanity has been entered. This detail should be a reminder that *Dracula* is a medical as well as a legal case, and that the former discipline struggles as much as the latter when attempting to comprehend the unprecedented phenomenon of the vampire. Where a legal case attempts to connect motivation and action with consequence, a medical case similarly reconstructs a credible pattern of cause and effect based upon symptomatology and pathology. The more popular meaning of case – that of a container or portmanteau – is also relevant here: a case should effectively contain the matter under study or discussion, explaining it so as to leave no query or unanswered question. The medical case study, in other words, is a form associated with both logic and rhetoric: in common with the legal case it is concerned with the appreciation and processing of evidence, observation and data. In *Dracula*, medicine, like the law, is not depicted as institutionally negligent, but is perceived, rather as an inflexible practice whose limitations are exposed as the narrative progresses.

If *Dracula* is a case study in anything, it is in the limitations of the unimaginative or rule-bound mind. Seward is depicted in the novel as an empiricist, a scientific thinker who develops a theory through experiment and observation. This is the whole basis of his treatment of Renfield: Seward provokes the lunatic with gifts of sugar and the offer of a cat, and closely observes the development of Renfield's obsession before formulating a general theory of mental deviance (111–14). Seward sees himself as an experimenter cast in the mould of the vivisectionists Sir John Burdon-Sanderson and David Ferrier, whose work he mentions in comparison to his own (115). Though he admits that in his manipulation of the lunatic there is 'something of cruelty' (102), an ethical conscience explicitly limits Seward's drift towards human, as opposed to animal, experimentation (114). His self-proclaimed medical radicalism and speculative foresight are, however, superficial, in that his interpretation of medical symptoms elsewhere in *Dracula* is both conservative and dogmatic.

Indeed, Seward is negligently dismissive of the symptoms displayed by Lucy, whose health is entrusted to him by his close friend Arthur Holmwood following her return from Whitby. Because of the irony constructed by the novel's structure, where the reader is aware of the Count's vampirism and his interest in both Whitby (65) and the environs of Seward's Purfleet asylum (64), the physician's misdiagnosis of the increasing pallor exhibited by his patient, is particularly visible. Logically, when Seward observes that 'the qualitative analysis' (155) of Lucy's blood gives no clue as to her pallor, the reader is implicitly prompted to query why he does not attempt to make a *quantitative* analysis: quality and quantity are rhetorically related, in layman's terms at least. If this were not enough, Seward dismisses the 'ragged, exhausted appearance' of the puncture wounds upon the vampirized Lucy's neck as not relevant to her progressive bloodlessness. His hasty dismissal is worth quoting at length. Seward recalls:

> It at once occurred to me that this wound, or whatever it was, might be the means of that manifest loss of blood; but I abandoned the idea as soon as formed, for such a thing could not be. The whole bed would have been drenched to a scarlet with the blood which the girl must have lost to leave such a pallor as she had before the transfusion. (167)

The irony of Seward's statement is vested in its rhetorical closeness to the blood transfusion he mentions in his final sentence. That transfusion has been enacted upon the same bed, and liquid blood has been taken from one circulation, via a puncture, to be injected into another without, one assumes, any spillage or staining of the sheets.[16]

Seward, who has hitherto attributed Lucy's deteriorating condition to 'something mental' (155) rather than to any physical cause, simply cannot see beyond that which conventional medicine tells him *ought* to be there. Seward's diagnosis is a matter of both professional bias and patriarchal prejudice. As an alienist, or physician of the abnormal mind, his practice leans towards psychological rather than physiological medicine. If the blood is not there, Seward's reasoning would implicitly suggest, it is most likely to have been lost in the conventional manner associated with women of Lucy's age – menstruation.[17] Menstruation, in the institutionally patriarchal gaze of late-Victorian medicine, was associated with hysteria, a debilitating mental condition exacerbated by sexual desire and the attentive presence of young men.[18] For Seward, Lucy's symptoms can suggest only one diagnosis.

The obvious, however, is true. The precedented and conventional patriarchal medicine which says that Lucy's debilitation must be a hysterical consequence of her age and impending marriage is in error. The physiological rather than psychological hypothesis is the correct one. Van Helsing, chiding his former pupil gently, makes this clear: 'You are clever man, friend John; you reason well and your wit is bold; but you are too prejudiced. You do not let your eyes see or your ears hear, and that which is outside your daily life is not of account to you' (234). Perversely, Mina Harker, an amateur rather than a professional, is the most uninhibited and flexible thinker in *Dracula*. She successfully adapts the criminal psychology of Lombroso and Nordau to the unprecedented case of Count Dracula (385), and thereby predicts his behaviour as successfully as that of any conventional criminal. Though it might be tempting to interpret Mina's comparative acuity with Stoker's rather complex attitude towards assertive women, it could as easily be argued that she emblematizes the novel's hostility towards professionalism and specialism. Mina, who is not bound by professional qualifications or courtesies, and Van Helsing, who is qualified in many fields, are the Count's most far-sighted and formidable opponents. Being capable of transcending the boundaries of dogma and methodology they are central to what Victor Sage terms the novel's 'elaborate attack on facile scepticism, purblind belief in "progress" and scientific materialism'.[19]

LANGUAGE AND DIALECT

As a documentary text, *Dracula* is regulated by the linguistic and grammatical controls associated with the respective conventions of the diary, the casebook, the letter and newspaper journalism. The novel does, however, embody a significant element of non-standard English. The function of both dialectal English and foreign-inflected registers of language in the novel goes beyond the simple need to provide 'local colour' in either Transylvania or London's East End. Language is a crucial icon of identity in the novel. A common language ensures not merely coherent and precise communication between its users but may also serve as a way to differentiate one group of language users from another. Communication is possible between such groups, though it may not always be accurate – and its grotesqueness may at times serve as the vehicle for prejudice or for humour. The reader is located at the point where these languages intersect, and is thus ideally placed to appreciate the ironies which arise when they meet in the tense space that is the novel's documentation.

The characters within *Dracula* may conveniently be divided into a number of linguistic groups: those who speak standard English; those whose English is inflected with the accent or grammar of some other language; and those who speak a dialectal variation of English. Standard English is spoken in the novel by only a small number of educated Britons – Arthur Holmwood, John Seward, Jonathan Harker and the two heroines. It proclaims both a central, nationalistic identity for the coalition against the Count, while still acknowledging how fractured that identity might be. The different educational attainments associated with a society divided by social class present particular opportunities for communication to break down. '*Omnia Romae venalia sunt*', or 'All Romans are venal' (102), Seward's untranslated allusion to Juvenal's *Satires,* might well be readily understood by Holmwood, the recipient of a Gentleman's education. It is less likely, though, to be immediately accessible to the bourgeois Harker. Van Helsing, notably, has elsewhere to explain the relevance of a subsequent Latin quotation – '*Festina Lente*', or 'make haste slowly' (345) – to the solicitor. The reader who can understand the Classical allusions is thus drawn into linguistic complicity with those who speak them. Those who cannot understand are temporarily excluded from community and communication.

The somewhat limited educational opportunities conventionally afforded to Victorian women might well make such Classical allusions inaccessible to them also. Mina, though, is again scripted as an exceptional polymath. Though her occupation as an 'assistant schoolmistress' (94) associates her with standard English, she is sufficiently educated so as to be able to aptly deploy the untranslated Latin phrase '*Omne ignotum pro magnifico*', or 'Everything, of which we are ignorant, must be something very fine' (360), in her personal journal. Elsewhere, Mina is sufficiently aware of her husband's professional idiom as to be able to correctly deploy the legal phrase 'hotch pot' (373), and she displays a similar facility with medical discourse through her use of Lombroso and Nordau (385–6). The professional idioms of medicine and law are effectively embedded within the English used by the alliance against the Count. Because she is able to understand them, albeit with a lay person's comprehension, Mina is an empowered and exceptional woman, though her position is undoubtedly restricted because of her sex. When Van Helsing applauds Mina's 'man's brain' (279) he is effectively acknowledging her felicity with gendered professional languages and thought-processes. For all this, however, he is quick to exclude her from the group's full confidence because, in such dangerous affairs, there is 'no part for a woman' (279).

English inflected with the accent or grammar of countries perceived as 'foreign' in *Dracula* is spoken by three central characters and a number of peripheral figures, most of the latter associated with the European lower classes. Quincey Morris, a Texan adventurer who has travelled with both Seward and Holmwood (103), is perhaps the most curious of the three. Lucy, notably, is captivated by Morris's use of an American slang which couples inaccurate biblical allusion with an equestrian motif redolent of the 'Wild West'.[20] As Lucy admits, however, Morris 'doesn't always speak slang' and, indeed, 'is really well educated and has exquisite manners' (99): his diction may well therefore be an affectation, emphasized for Lucy's benefit. Morris's speech, though, does differentiate him somewhat from those who never have recourse to non-standard English in the novel and, as Franco Moretti and Andrew Smith have argued, this effectively associates him with the invading Count. Whether or not *Dracula* represents the political fable envisaged by Moretti and Smith, where Britain is as unprepared to counter the rise of the United States as it is to oppose the subtle individual invasion of the vampire, is irrelevant here.[21] When Lucy (100) and Mina (385) briefly quote Morris's Americanisms, they symbolically move away from the linguistic purity of their immediate social circle. In effect, they become assimilated with the cultural and linguistic Other enforced here by the American's idiolect, but elsewhere by the Count's penetrative and infectious bite.

Where American English merely disrupts Morris's racial association with his British counterparts, Van Helsing's characteristically broken English consistently accentuates his unfeigned foreignness. The Roman Catholic Dutchman's assimilation into the Protestant, Anglo-Saxon coalition against the Count is underpinned by his proficiency in the transcendent professional languages of law and medicine, and also in his comprehension of a vision of Christianity which makes sectarian differences irrelevant. Van Helsing's speech is at times a source of sporadic humour: his rendering of Holmwood's formal fox-hunting attire as an incongruous 'red frock' (357), for example, defamiliarizes a common icon of upper-class rural life.

At times, though, the irony of Van Helsing's curious speech mobilizes a dialogue between the literal and the figurative in *Dracula*. This is at its most pointed in the Dutchman's account of the vampire's departure from London on the *Czarina Catherine*. There is an undoubted comedic value vested in both Van Helsing's inability to wholly comprehend the British expletives 'bloody' and 'blooming', and his insistent repetition of them in such a way as to undermine their value as conventional swear words. Thus, when the ship's captain insists that the Count 'had better be quick – with blood – for that his ship will leave the place – of blood – before the turn of the tide – with blood' (361), the novel's emphasis is deflected towards the *literal* presence of blood upon the ship. The irony of the ship's captain's words is dependent upon his ignorance of the occult nature of his passenger, but the tension between the literal and figurative is a context that would surely not be lost upon a native speaker of English. In *Dracula*, as Victor Sage asserts, blood is 'a grotesque pun': its multiple meanings, though, depend on the ironies that arise between its function in the various linguistic registers, national and professional, that structure Stoker's novel.[22] Much of its contextual grotesqueness, though, depends upon Van Helsing's inability to clearly express himself through the English language.

Count Dracula's imperfect command of the English language has different implications, however. The Count speaks considerably less than the other major characters, and is effectively narrated, recollected or interpreted throughout by others. Only in one letter to Jonathan Harker does the vampire command words in his own right (44), and even this document is doubly compromised in that it is first reproduced in Harker's journal and then subsequently transcribed by Mina. The Count's difficulties with the English language mark his status not merely as an outsider, but also as a parvenu, and a foreigner who aspires to Englishness. The Count is explicit regarding his aspirations, asking Harker from the outset to correct any mistakes in his diction (61). As he explains to the solicitor,

Well I know that, did I move and speak in your London, none there are who would not know me for a stranger. That is not enough for me. Here I am noble; I am boyar; the common people know me, and I am master. But a stranger in a strange land, he is no one; men know him not – and to know not is to care not for. I am content if I am like the rest, so that no man stops if he see me, or pause in his speaking if he hear my words, to say 'Ha! ha! a stranger'. (61)

There is duplicity in the Count's closing statement: anonymity and invisibility, rather than noteworthiness, is the key to the vampire's subtle imperial mission among the 'teeming millions' (92) of London. A stranger is more visible than a native, and 'care' in this context implies unwelcome attention. The Count's book-learning, though, can provide him only with the letter rather than the spirit of an English – or Western – identity. His assimilation is shallow, and quite at odds with the unavoidable signifiers of his body. In Piccadilly, the Count may at first sight appear to be nothing more than, in the words of Mina Harker, 'a tall, thin man, with a beaky nose and black moustache and pointed beard', though she is forced to recognize that 'His face was not a good face; it was hard, and cruel, and sensual, and his big white teeth . . . were pointed like an animal's' (215). Education and clothing do not make an Englishman, and the Count's progressive loss of control following his discovery in London is signified finally by his appearance on the *Czarina Catherine* wearing 'a hat of straw that suit not him or the time' (360). At this point all pretence of Englishness has been dropped: if the Captain may not immediately recognize the Count as a Transylvanian vampire, he is quick to associate him with that conventional demon of British insular xenophobia, the Frenchman (361).

The Count's irregular English is a sign not merely of his foreignness but also a specific indicator of his approximate and imperfect assimilation to the national culture of Great Britain. This incomplete affiliation links him to another significant group of Othered characters in *Dracula*, the British working classes. The dialect-speaking working classes are not, in effect, full citizens. Their social disability goes beyond the political advantages granted by the right to vote. Essentially, they cannot communicate efficiently or effectively with those who broker the wealth and power of the nation, and their words and their writings are apt to lead to misunderstanding. They are subject beings, to be variously used by the Count and his opponents, and they are invariably narrated, their words (and linguistic peculiarities) always being represented or embedded within the accounts of others. The potential affiliation between the vampire and the London working classes as incomplete citizens of the nation is further underscored by the characteristic thirst exhibited by both: where the vampire desires blood, the British working man seems to find satisfaction only in 'a stiff glass of grog, or rather more of the same' (200). If the vampire, as a criminally insane degenerate (385) finds a ready ally in the homicidal lunatic, Renfield (346), he may as easily find assistance as well as a larder among the thirsty, selfish, small-minded proletariat (385).

In London, the zoo-keeper Thomas Bilder is perhaps the best spoken of those in non-professional employment, though his phonetic cockneyisms – he talks of 'perfeshunal subjects' (179) and 'kawffee' (180) – contrast with the standard English spoken by the *Pall Mall Gazette* reporter who interviews him. Bilder is, though, deferential to the Count, because the latter's association with wolves may make him 'a good friend to keepers' (181). Though Bilder does not take payment from the vampire, other working men do – specifically the 'three loafers' (307) who assist him to move his coffins into the Piccadilly mansion, and the carters who redistributed the boxes to the various London locations. These latter again enjoy a Dickensian richness of diction: the aitch is characteristically dropped in conversation, and W subsitutes for V, most notably in the affection of 'wery' (304) for 'very'.[23] This peculiar speech inhibits efficient communication between the educated and working classes: Harker is confused by the phonetic spelling used by one of his informants, only gradually coming to understand that 'Poters Cort' is in fact 'Potter's Court', and Korkrans (or Corcoran's) Lodging House is managed by a 'deputy' rather than a 'depite' (305–6). The denizens of proletarian London may be as difficult to understand as the peasants Harker encounters earlier in Bistritz: indeed, the solicitor is perversely at a disadvantage in his own country, as he lacks the polyglot dictionary which enables him to clarify the 'queer words' repeated by the European peasantry (46).

Mina Harker and Lucy Westenra encounter similar difficulties when listening to the Whitby mariners, the other dialectal group encountered in the novel. Again, a speaker of relatively standard English, the Coastguard, is strategically deployed in order to provide a contrast (118–19). The Mariners, though, do not share the thirst of their urban counterparts, nor do they find themselves the ready employees of the invading Count. The colourful Whitby dialect spoken by Mr Swales and his seafaring associates is rendered almost fondly in the novel, and serves to mark the speakers as old-fashioned, provincial and, perversely, more concerned with spirit than appetite. Swales's *danse macabre* imagery of 'tombsteans' and 'death-sarks' (108) may appear sceptical at the outset, as Mina indeed concludes (106), but it is succeeded by a homily on mortality, where the mariner contends that 'death be all that we can rightly depend on' (118). The irony of his words should be obvious to the reader, who has already seen a dead man walk in Harker's account: the old-fashioned spirituality of provincial England is as ill-equipped to deal with the unprecedented incursion of the vampire as the enlightened empiricism of the metropolitan professional classes. In a sense, neither has adequate words through which to conceptualize the vampire.

SUGGESTIONS FOR FURTHER ANALYSIS

Stoker's fiction beyond *Dracula* is punctuated by numerous dialects and professional languages. Much of Stoker's less-known work has returned to print in recent years, and its ready availability will provide many opportunities for comparison with the linguistic groupings depicted in *Dracula*. There are dialect speakers, in particular, in *The Snake's Pass* (1890), which is set in the west of Ireland; and within *The Watter's Mou'* (1894), *The Mystery of the Sea* (1902) and *Lady*

Athlyne (1908), all of which employ Scottish settings. *The Lady of the Shroud* (1909), a *faux* vampire novel set in the Edwardian Balkans, further juxtaposes the peasantry of Scotland and Eastern Europe. The language of professional men, too, informs the plot of *The Jewel of Seven Stars* (1903), which is narrated by a barrister who encounters, among others, a physician, an Egyptologist and a detective. American characters and transatlantic diction feature strongly in *Lady Athlyne* and *The Shoulder of Shasta* (1895), while Stoker's long essay on the culture of the United States, *A Glimpse of America* (1886) is a rich repository of contextual material regarding both nationality and gender.

These works provide useful comparative material from Stoker's own writings which will support the linguistic and stylistic analysis of *Dracula*, though only *The Lady of the Shroud* clearly recalls that novel's epistolary and documentary structure. Taking *Dracula* in a broader Victorian context, particular comparisons may be made, as Stoker's reviewers suggested, to the works of Wilkie Collins. Beyond the epistolary and documentary structure that aligns *Dracula* with *The Moonstone* and *The Woman in White* lie a number of comparable fictionalizations of racial difference, social status and mental responsibility. The Indians who seek to recover the titular Moonstone in Collins's novel have been depicted in criticism as foreign invaders, and their occult-inflected treatment of the English boy whom they utilize as an aid in divination might be further deployed as a counterpart to the vampire's physical and hypnotic proprietorship of both Lucy and Mina.[24] Mark Hennelly (1982) has drawn credible comparisons between Count Fosco in *The Woman in White* and Stoker's Count Dracula, though there is more to be said with regard to the mental patients closely associated with these two manipulative figures.[25] It is not so much the style of speech employed by Anne Catherick and R. M. Renfield that links the two incarcerated lunatics, but rather the value attributed to their pronouncements: key data, delivered from their lips, may be dismissed out of hand or tentatively acknowledged, but it never attains the value of those who are legally free but ironically less informed than the incarcerated. Renfield's social respectability, in particular, is negated by his lunacy: his words hold less import than a working-class carter's. The same might be said of the complaints issued by Collins's Laura, Lady Glyde, once she is incarcerated in Catherick's place. The status of the speaker modifies the power and value of their utterances.

Finally, it is important to consider the relationship between *Dracula* and the Gothic, taking the latter as both a generic matrix and as a focus for criticism. Critics, certainly, have long acknowledged the eighteenth- and nineteenth-century Gothic antecedents of Stoker's geographical locations, edifices and plot scenarios. Though Gothic was for many years dismissed by the critical establishment as little more than a literary curiosity or a form of hack writing, the genre has come to prominence as a critical preoccupation in recent years. Though this has precipitated the status of *Dracula* from a work of fantasy to an index of social, sexual and political concern, it has also to a certain extent marginalized other discernible literary influences upon the novel. Stoker's fiction, including and beyond *Dracula*, embodies elements characteristic of the detective narrative, of the romance and of early science fiction. The work is essentially a hybrid, yet readings of the novel as a Gothic exemplar continue to predominate in criticism. One might profitably query, therefore, why this has come to be the case, and, indeed, whether the predominance of Gothic has unduly limited what might be said about *Dracula*.

CHAPTER 3

READING *DRACULA*

DRACULA IN CRITICISM

Dracula has attracted the attention of a remarkable breadth of critical and theoretical approaches over the past 50 years. These range from the most orthodox of 1970s Freudian interpretations to the acerbic historicist rejections of psychoanalysis characteristic of the 1990s, and encompass the intellectual shifts that have blurred the boundaries between feminism and gender studies, and between literary criticism and cultural studies.[1] As a practice, *Dracula* criticism is intensely self-referential. It is arguably as preoccupied with earlier critical commentary upon the novel as it is with the actual content of *Dracula* itself. There is no linear pattern of evolution or development in criticism of Stoker's novel, where, for example, cultural materialism might be seen to succeed psychoanalysis, or feminism to yield to a broader approach through gender studies. Like the vampire, *Dracula* criticism defies time and chronology: it is simultaneously anachronistic and contemporary, in the sense that new interpretations of Stoker's novel tend to explicitly parallel, supplement or commentate upon their predecessors while never enforcing a satisfactory closure upon the influence of those earlier critics.

As evidence for this, one need only consider two statements made almost 40 years apart, by Maurice Richardson in 'The Psychoanalysis of Ghost Stories' (1959) and Robert Mighall in 'Sex, History and the Vampire' (1998), respectively. Writing at the very beginning of *Dracula* criticism, Richardson contends that the novel *must* be read 'From a Freudian standpoint' because 'from no other does the story make any sense'. The vampire, and thus the novel, in other words, represent nothing more than the coded expression of a repressed, unspeakable sexuality.[2] Mighall, no doubt mindful of rhetorical closures such as this, is fully prepared to concede that 'Modern criticism' insists upon the presence of 'some "deeper" sexual secret' behind the 'supernatural phenomena' of *Dracula*. That '"deeper" sexual secret', though, is for Mighall *not* Victorian but wholly twentieth century: the preoccupations of post-Freudian criticism, in other words, are being read in the place of anything that the vampire *might* have meant to a Victorian reader. Perversely, while it seeks to dispel the currency of psychoanalytical or sexual interpretations of *Dracula*, Mighall's own rhetoric perpetuates their influence. Simply by naming critics committed to exposing the alleged, coded sexuality vested in the Count, Mighall ironically lends them a semblance of authority, intruding their supposedly anachronistic presence into his critical present, and perpetuating their place in the canon of *Dracula* criticism.[3] Arguably, a reader in the twenty-first century is as likely to find Richardson and his psychoanalytical successors within a recent critical study of *Dracula* as he or she is to encounter Mighall and his contemporaries.

The enduring intensity of this critical cross-referencing is largely a consequence of the manner in which the early criticism of *Dracula* deployed the novel's incidents and components. More recent critics are for the most part careful to locate *Dracula* within historical, cultural, generic or documented biographical contexts. The earliest critics of the novel, however, frequently took its incidents and perceived symbolism almost in isolation, reading them often simplistically as, for the most part, timeless, self-sufficient and obvious signifiers of a repressed sexuality. The result was an undue reliance not merely upon sexuality as the apparent 'key' to *Dracula*, but also a critical concentration upon a relatively limited number of evocative scenes within the novel. These scenes – and, often, the sexual interpretations and the critics first associated with them – have subsequently come to be deployed as evidence even where sexuality is not the critical focus.

To recall but one, very obvious, example, the evocative substance that is blood in *Dracula* has attracted a phenomenal range of symbolic interpretations. Many of these, of course, are avowedly sexual. Maurice Richardson, for example, is an orthodox Freudian in his suggestion that blood is an unconscious symbolic substitute for semen in *Dracula*, where Peter Redgrove and Penelope Shuttle's suggestion, in *The Wise Wound: Menstruation and Everywoman* (1978), that the fluid subliminally recalls menstrual discharge may be seen as a logical development from the phallocentrism of early psychoanalysis.[4] The influence of Richardson is, not surprisingly, evident in C. F. Bentley's influential 1972 study 'The Monster in the Bedroom: Sexual Symbolism in Bram Stoker's *Dracula*', even though that work's theoretical orientation veers away from the psychoanalytical dogmatism of 'The Psychoanalysis of Ghost Stories'.[5] However, even where the literal – rather than symbolic – implications of blood form the focus of analysis, sexual symbolism and critics of sexuality appear to be necessarily invoked as a reference point. In a 1989 article otherwise concerned with the physiological processes of blood transfusion, for example, David Hume Flood seems compelled to acknowledge Bentley. Again, in *Beyond Dracula: Bram Stoker's Fiction and Its Cultural Context* (2000), William Hughes acknowledges the sexual interpretations advanced by several other critics in a reading of how blood may function as a signifier of linage, family and race.[6] Neither of these works is preoccupied with sexuality. Thus, as Christopher Craft observes, 'Modern critical accounts of *Dracula* . . . almost universally agree that vampirism both expresses and distorts an originally sexual energy', so that, in the words of Jennifer Wicke, 'It is not possible to write about *Dracula* without raising the sexual issue.'[7]

All of these critical studies, to a greater or lesser degree, deploy a common range of incidents as evidence, as indeed do many others less concerned with the symbolics of blood. There is a tendency in *Dracula* criticism, in other words, to reinterpret the same material from the novel rather than to develop new focuses for criticism – and *Dracula* criticism will be richer when critics consider at length and without prejudice the minor characters and less-explored scenarios of Stoker's work. For the moment, the only satisfactory way to adequately demonstrate the variety and breadth of critical commentary upon *Dracula* is to take the scenes customarily regarded as being central to criticism and view them in all their critical plurality. These central scenes are, in order of their appearance in the novel: the depiction of face of Count Dracula, as observed by Jonathan Harker (chapter 2); the attempted 'seduction' of Harker by the three female vampires (chapter 3); the staking and 'death' of Lucy Westenra (chapter 16); the Count's attack upon Mina Harker (chapter 21); and – more disparate, in that it is scattered across the extent of the novel – the cohesion of the coalition against Count Dracula. Though often cited and quoted, these scenes do not exist in isolation. Rather, in criticism they have become the central reference points for other events intimately related to their implications, perceived symbolism and narrative consequences. Thus, Jonathan Harker's account of Count Dracula's face is intimate to Mina Harker's 'scientific' reading of the vampire's character in chapter 25, just as Lucy's trance existence, before and after her conversion to vampirism, is relevant to the Count's attack upon Mina. These four specific scenes, and the concept of the alliance against the vampire, are, as it were, the staples of *Dracula*'s critical repertoire – and the pre-existing foundations upon which new interpretations have so often been raised.

THE PHYSIOGNOMY OF COUNT DRACULA

Vampirism, as a psychoanalytically taboo practice, has become a preoccupation in the study of *Dracula* to such an extent that the work's alleged unconscious symbolism is often emphasized at the expense of the detail contained within the novel itself.[8] In committed psychoanalytical readings, Count Dracula is seldom the distinctive figure depicted in detail at the inception of the novel by Jonathan Harker. He seems to lose his physicality, to be defined only by his actions and their interpretation, to become wholly bound up in the interpretative processes of the twentieth- and twenty-first centuries. The *nineteenth* century, though, is the context of Harker's description of the vampire, and so the Count, though apparently a fifteenth-century warlord, is presented to the reader in language that is implicated within the interpretative processes of late-Victorian Britain. Harker's description of the Count, written following his first night in Castle Dracula, thus represents an intelligent Victorian layman's simultaneous observation (and, therefore, unspoken interpretation) of the physiology and physiognomy of his host. Harker's description, though, is not shaped by a knowledge of the Count's vampirism: it is, in other words, an interpretation of the Count as if he were a conventional human being, and thus represents an attempt to extract a sense of individual character from the raw data of appearance.

Throughout his journey to Castle Dracula, Harker is depicted as an obsessive documenter of facts and details: he records regional dishes such as 'paprika hendl' (41) and 'mamaliga' (43), and comments upon the curious (and, to him, immodest) fashions adopted by the younger peasant women (43) and the elderly innkeeper's wife (44). Elsewhere, significantly, he recalls how the foreign peasants he encounters appear prone to disease as well as superstition, for 'goitre was painfully prevalent' in Transylvania (48). Even at this early stage, the body, and things intimately associated with the body, such as clothing and decorations, have begun to serve a function: they signify not merely difference, but also the presence of comparative inferiority or degeneration when placed rhetorically next to the modesty of English dress or the disease-free perfection of the English body. Harker's description of the Count must therefore be taken in the context of his protracted observation of the European peasantry. The fact that he devotes so much time, and advances so much detail when recalling his host's appearance and behaviour indicates not merely the Count's importance as the client of his employer, but also how alien, and indeed unusual, he appears to the obsessive solicitor.

Harker, restored by his own admission to his 'normal state' (57) of mental equilibrium after the confusion of his night-time journey through the Borgo Pass, takes pains to describe his reassuringly 'courteous' (57) host:

> His face was a strong – a very strong – aquiline, with high bridge of the thin nose and peculiarly arched nostrils; with lofty domed forehead, and hair growing scantily round the temples but profusely elsewhere. His eyebrows were very massive, almost meeting over the nose, and with bushy hair that seemed to curl in its own profusion. The mouth, so far as I could see it under the heavy moustache, was fixed and rather cruel-looking, with peculiarly sharp white teeth; these protruded over the lips, whose remarkable ruddiness showed astonishing vitality in a man of his years. For the rest, his ears were pale, and at the tops extremely pointed; the chin was broad and strong, and the cheeks firm though thin. The general effect was one of extraordinary pallor. (58)

The Count is clearly signalled as exceptional here, through Harker's insistent use of adjectives such as 'peculiarly', remarkable', 'astonishing', 'extremely' and 'extraordinary'. There is a *frisson* of unease here, also, as the Count's age and bloodlessness sit uneasily next to his latent strength and obvious forcefulness. A Victorian reader familiar with even the most basic conventions of physiognomy – the study of character through facial features – would no doubt concur, also, that the 'sharp white teeth' and 'fixed and rather cruel-looking' mouth involuntarily indicate violent qualities held in check by an urbane and civilized veneer. The enduring presence of these qualities is indeed subsequently confirmed by the Count's recollections of historical and racial events, the wars and invasions (69–71) recounted 'as if he had been present at them all' (69). With the vampire viewed here as a mortal, Harker and his reader might well be forgiven for accepting a seemingly self-evident relationship between face and character: the Count is aggressive, proud, arbitrary and exceptional, no doubt, but can hardly be considered unprecedented at this juncture.

There is more at stake here than shallow symbolism, however. The parlour game of physiognomy was intimately related to more serious quasi-medical practices which interpreted the mind through the body. Dismissed today as pseudosciences, these practices – which included phrenology, craniology and mesmerism – enjoyed a fluctuating currency across the nineteenth century. They are well documented in recent scholarship, but were for the most part ignored or dismissed as ephemeral in criticism published before the 1980s.[9] Harker's account of his host has been undoubtedly shaped by one of the late-Victorian pseudosciences, the so-called scientific criminology popularized by Cesare Lombroso (1836–1909) and Max Nordau (1849–1923). If the Victorian reader did not immediately recognize the conventions deployed in Harker's implicit assessment of the Count, their relevance would likely have become clear in retrospect once Harker's wife had depicted the Count as 'a criminal and of criminal type', for 'Nordau and Lombroso would so classify him' (385).

The factor which allows the theory to be applied to a figure who is successively perceived as being conventionally mortal and satanically immortal is not criminality specifically, but rather the association made by both Lombroso and Nordau between antisocial actions and mental deviance. Mina's recourse to Nordau and Lombroso follows Van Helsing's depiction of criminality as a form of mental disability, which concludes that the criminal 'be not of man-stature as to brain' (384). Van Helsing's opinion, too, is in keeping with Lombroso's thought, though Harker's earlier description of the Count recalls also the Italian criminologist's assertion that actual or potential antisocial qualities could be discerned through reference to the shape and development of an individual's body. If criminality represents an antisocial degeneration from the moral and behavioural standards expected by modern society, the criminal's body may by association represent a reversion to a more primitive form of humanity. Like the vampire, the criminal is an intrusion of the past into the present.

Writing in 1975, Leonard Wolf noted briefly that Harker's description of the Count embodied some of the facial characteristics popularly associated with Lombroso's predestined criminal.[10] The extent to which this facial resemblance also implicated the text within the assumptions of Victorian psychology, though, remained undeveloped until the publication of Ernest Fontana's pioneering article 'Lombroso's Criminal Man and Stoker's *Dracula*' in 1985. Fontana's succinct and convincing tabulation of the interplay between Lombroso's criminal theory and the depiction of Stoker's vampire is worth quoting at length:

> Dracula's 'aquiline nose', 'massive' eyebrows, and 'pointed ears' correspond to characteristics identified by Lombroso: 'the nose is often aquiline like the beak of a bird of prey'; the eyebrows are generally bushy in murderers and violators of women and 'tend to meet across the nose'; and there is 'a protuberance on the upper part of the posterior margin' of the ear, 'a relic of the pointed ear characteristic of apes'. . . . His 'peculiarly sharp white teeth' that protrude over his lips correspond to Lombroso's observation that a criminal often has 'supernumerary teeth . . . and often 'strongly developed canines'.[11]

Further, as Fontana points out, by way of a telling quotation from Lombroso, the criminal is 'an atavistic being, the relic of a vanished race'. An atavist bears a closer moral or physical resemblance to his or her ancestors than to the present generation. As Daniel Pick argues, in a later exploration of *Dracula* in the context of degenerationist theory, the atavist as degenerate 'was cast as a kind of social vampire who corrupted the nation'. The mortal atavist did not inhabit the towers of ancient castles but rather the dark spaces of the modern city: as the proletarian slum dweller or criminal underclass, its vampirism was vested not in a literal draining of blood but in the perceived undermining of healthy bodies and healthy morals. Quite simply, the late-Victorian urban underclass was perceived as being on the point of overwhelming bourgeois civilization with a flood of fertile, degenerate offspring, thus draining both its vitality and imperilling its ascendancy.[12]

The threat posed by the fictional vampire thus extends beyond the immediate risk of fatal, individual predation associated with his own presence. The vampire as occult figure, and the vampire as social metaphor, fuse easily in context. The possibility that the Count might assimilate with 'degenerate' elements already present within the culture he has travelled to multiplies his capacity to do harm in the present. Their reproduction, whether achieved sexually or vampirically, signals further the perpetuation of degeneration into the future. Fontana continues:

> Dracula is a threat to societies of predominantly morally and socially evolved humanity, because there survives within these societies, even in England, a minority of potentially 'diseased' individuals who are driven, subconsciously, to a reversion back to the atavistic, pre-civilized world from which Dracula survives, and who, subconsciously, 'bid him to come', and who become, for Dracula, 'flesh of my flesh, blood of my blood, kin of my kin [331]'.[13]

So, just as the vampire has historically predated upon the diseased and superstitiously backward-looking Transylvanian peasantry, he is now able to avail himself of their equivalent within modern Britain.

The Count's first victim upon British soil, however, is not working class. Lucy Westenra is an heiress, socially privileged enough to be courted successively by a wealthy physician, an American landowner and a British nobleman. Degeneration, though, is no respecter of social advantage. Lucy is explicitly identified as a sleepwalker and, indeed, her deceased father 'had the same habit' (116). Under the gaze of degenerationist theory, though, sleepwalking is not a habit, but a pathological medical condition, and one which indicates a departure from the norm. Its presence associates the sleepwalker with other more spectacular forms of mental incapacity, such as susceptibility to hypnosis, hysteria or even madness.[14] She is sufficiently aligned to the abnormal to make her an easy and appropriate victim for the vampire.[15] Notably, when Lucy descends into active vampirism the focus of her predation echoes the paradigm established by Count Dracula in Eastern Europe. Her first victims are the children of the British urban proletariat: notably their speech, in which she becomes not the 'beautiful' but the 'bloofer lady' (220–1) is as alien to standard pronunciation as anything spoken in the broken English of Germany or Romania. They are not full members of the nation.

The Count's face is, however, not the face of an *indigenous* degenerate. The question thus arises as to why, with his imperfect language skills and deficient social graces only partially improved by Harker's example, the Count is not readily detected in London, where he is observed several times in broad daylight (215, 346, 348). The answer is that London, by the end of the nineteenth century, was already a multicultural and multiracial city, and so foreigners were far less visible *as aliens* than the Count himself might have anticipated while still in Transylvania. Immigrants, temporary residents and refugees lived in close conjunction with their indigenous Anglo-Saxon neighbours in the slums of London and other cities. The perceived decline of the indigenous working-class population thus became further associated with a persistent cultural fear that immigrant populations were variously challenging, besieging or even colonizing not merely indigenous communities but even the very bodies of which they were constructed. Sexual encounters, mixed marriages and religious conversions potentially undermine the integrity of the Anglo-Saxon race and, as Stephen D. Arata suggests, a popular view arose that 'Miscegenation leads, not to the mixing of races, but to the biological and political annihilation of the weaker race by the stronger.'[15] The fear, implicitly, is that the Anglo-Saxon race is not the stronger. The primitive and the atavistic, as seemingly demonstrated in late-Victorian works such as Rudyard Kipling's 'The Mark of the Beast' (1890) or Richard Marsh's *The Beetle* (1897), may overwhelm enervated modernity, transforming the self and weakening the race and the nation in the process. Acknowledging the racial – and racist – political hysteria characteristic of the period, several critics have come to read *Dracula* as a form of imperial parable, a fantasy, as it were, of reverse colonization on a par with H. Rider Haggard's *She* (1887) or H. G. Wells's *The War of the Worlds* (1898).[16]

Stephen D. Arata's 'The Occidental Tourist: *Dracula* and the Anxiety of Reverse Colonization' (1990) is perhaps the most influential of these readings. Arata argues that

> the Count can threaten the integrity of the nation precisely because of the nature of his threat to personal integrity. His attacks involve more than an assault on the isolated self, the subversion and loss of one's individual identity . . . Dracula imperils not merely his victims' personal identities, but also their cultural, political and racial selves. In *Dracula*, vampirism designates a kind of colonization of the body. Horror arises not because Dracula destroys bodies, but because he appropriates and transforms them. Having yielded

to his assault, one literally 'goes native' by becoming a vampire oneself.[17]

This is a credible reading, and Arata – and several of his successors – are quick to see in the vampire an allegory of mass-migration to England from the Balkan East generally, and from Romania in particular.[18] However, there is no suggestion that the Count's physiognomy represents a distinctively *Balkan* face, as might be depicted in the political cartoons or travel writings of the day. It is, though, an *Eastern* face, and one which might be contextually regarded as being so domesticated as to be unexceptionable in a British urban context: indeed, as a cliché, it appears more than once in *Dracula*, albeit in lesser detail and transferred from London to the eastern European port of Galatz.

As well as being described in detail by Jonathan Harker, and in passing by Mina, the Count is also recalled by the zoo-keeper Thomas Bilder, who encounters 'a tall, thin chap, with a ''ook nose and a pointed beard' (181). The emphasis upon the Count's nose is the factor which links him to another perceived foreign invader of the last quarter of the nineteenth century, the eastern European Jew. Britain was the destination of choice for many Jews fleeing the pogroms of Russia, Romania and the Austrian Empire. This resettlement caused friction with the indigenous working-class population, among whom they settled in London's Whitechapel in particular, and claims were made that the immigrants were displacing Christian East End residents and, as sweatshop employers, undermining wages and conditions in the local labour market.[19] Anti-Semitic prejudice was not confined to the working classes, however. If the residents of the poorer streets of London resented the archetypal Jewish corner-shop pawnbroker as a parasite, then more educated Britons retained a suspicion of the involvement of wealthier Jews in international banking, finance and stock broking.[20] The image of the vampire is an easy metaphor for such professions – indeed, Stoker was to depict an Irish moneylender in *The Snake's Pass* (1890), his first novel, as one who would 'take the blood out of yer body if he could sell it or use in anyhow!'[21]

If Dracula may be read as the representation of a Jew, then he arguably reflects the contextual fears of both the reactionary proletariat and the educated bourgeoisie. The Count hoards money – 'a great heap of gold . . . covered with a film of dust' (88) – in Transylvania, and figuratively bleeds 'a stream of gold' (349) when cut by Jonathan Harker in London. As an immigrant to Britain, he colonizes, purchasing houses in respectable suburbs such as Purfleet (64), in the very centre of the Metropolis at Piccadilly (306), and in the working-class districts of Mile End and Bermondsey (304). He is intimate with the bodies of native women, and those who fall under his control are, like sweated labour, little more than 'my creatures, to do my bidding' (350). He retains international contacts, and his finances purchase for him the allegiance of Szgany (82) and cockney (307) alike, just as much as they secure the services of a British solicitor and the protection of English law (336). Indeed, the only way that the vampire's opponents may successfully counter him is to mirror his policy of bribery and purchase, as Harker does when questioning the Count's former employees in Walworth (304) and Poplar (306), and Morris the dockyard staff at Doolittle's Wharf (360). Subtly, he has colonized his opponents too, inflecting their gentlemanly Christian culture with his Semitic mercantilism. He has not become satisfactorily English – but he has, in many respects, diluted the Englishness of those he has encountered, whether as victims, unknowing associates or conscious opponents.

There is one literal and unequivocal – though still heavily clichéd – Jew depicted in *Dracula*, and his explicit cultural associations arguably provide an additional index to the Count's place within popular British anti-Semitism. In the Romanian port of Galatz, Harker, Seward and Van Helsing meet with the Count's European shipping agent, Immanuel Hildesheim, 'a Hebrew of rather the Adelphi Theatre type, with a nose like a sheep, and a fez' (392). Carol Davison describes this as 'a distinctively Jewish physiognomy', but passes over the reference to the Adelphi Theatre in London's Strand, which specialized in melodrama and farce. Her central reference point for the physiognomy of both Hildesheim and Dracula is Henry Irving's stage portrayals of Shylock in *The Merchant of Venice* at the Lyceum Theatre, also on the Strand. A strong case, however, might be made for a more direct precursor to the Count within Beerbohm Tree's villainous Jewish hypnotist, Svengali, in the 1895 production of Paul Potter's *Trilby* at London's Haymarket Theatre.[22]

Though the connection between Svengali and Dracula was asserted by Nina Auerbach as early as 1981, criticism has tended to concentrate upon the 1894 novel of the same name by George du Maurier rather than the stage play. Stoker knew du Maurier socially, and would, as a theatrical professional, have been fully aware of Tree's highly successful production. The potential influence of the play, therefore, ought to be acknowledged: if the Count is not strictly a theatrical villain, the encounters in which he is presented as a character at the focus of a multiple gaze – most notably when he is disturbed in an ambiguously sexual embrace with Mina (325–6), or when he is held at bay by his opponents in Piccadilly (348–9) – recall the set tableaux of melodrama. *Dracula*, like *Trilby*, may well have been written with an eye for a spectacular future dramatization – though this was never realized in Stoker's lifetime.[23]

Though du Maurier's dark-bearded Svengali, a man of an uncertain age between 30 and 45, is hardly an immediate physical prototype for Stoker's Count, the two do share the distinction of a 'bony' frame (181), a pale or 'sallow' face (58), 'brilliant' or striking eyes (80), and 'a mongrel canine snarl' (58).[24] Svengali, moreover, comes 'out of the mysterious East! The poisonous East – birthplace and home of an ill wind that blows nobody good', and speaks one language with the accent of another; there is even something about his copious hair in particular that is 'offensive to the *normal* Englishman' (my italics).[25] He is an Othered figure, imperfectly integrated into the society in which he now moves, and associated therein with money, with dishonesty and with entrapment.

It is not these mere physical attributes, that link Svengali most forcefully to Stoker's Count, however. Svengali is, crucially, a mesmerist, a non-clinical practitioner of an early form of hypnotism, associated with mind-reading and thought transference. His manner of inducing a trance in Trilby is somewhat reminiscent of Van Helsing's attempts to gain access to the blood-based hypnotic control over Mina established by the Count on the night the group begins to destroy his coffins (331). Svengali hypnotizes Trilby through hand gestures, 'little passes and counterpasses on her forehead and temples and down her cheek and neck', just as Van Helsing 'commenced to make passes in front of [Mina], from over the top of her head downward, with each hand in turn' (355). Van Helsing seeks to read Mina's mind – or, rather, to experience the Count's own senses through the medium of Mina. Svengali and the Count, though, impose *their* respective versions of mesmerism in order to appropriate and control the wills and bodies of their female victims. In Svengali's case, this takes the form of training and conditioning her tuneless voice into that of an operatic diva. In this exploitation of a woman reduced to a commercial product there is a suggestion, as Davison notes, of prostitution of art if not of the actual body, another cliché apparently associated with the rapacious Jewish male.[26] Trilby's dual life, divided between the waking tuneless heroine and the mesmerized diva resembles the twofold, vampirized existences of both Lucy and Mina – all three are aware of their alternate selves incompletely (155, 204), if at all (389). Control, though, means ownership. When Count Dracula inducts Mina into vampirism, the sonorous incantation that proclaims her 'flesh of my flesh, blood of my blood, kin of my kin' (331) represents an obvious allusion to the rites of Christian marriage: Svengali, notably, introduces the singer he has created out of Trilby O'Ferrall to the world as La Svengali and she is, for others, Madame Svengali.[27] It is noteworthy, though, that Mina rationalizes her 'marriage' to the Count in images of 'shame' and 'polluted flesh' (340): it is the physical contact with the Count, the intimacies he has taken with her, that transform this representation of miscegenation into an issue of outrage.

The body of Count Dracula is thus arguably as important to the novel as his actions. It is a polemical body, and a focus for the novel's racial, sexual and moral Otherings. Variously degenerate or Jewish, the Count's face exhibits the unacceptable and antisocial moralities his body pursues. That body, as the body of an immigrant, maintains a crucial role in the demarcation process that allows the vampire hunters to impose upon him a form of justice and retribution that they could not so readily apply to one of their own. The body of the Count circulates within the body politic, and the bodies that make up the nation retain the liquid capacity to ultimately circulate within the vampire's own corporeal confines. All of the central characters are intimate with the Count's body. It is not merely that they come to resemble him by their actions, their bribery, their meting out of an arbitrary justice not sanctioned by modern law. As the Count boasts to his male opponents, 'Your girls that you all love are mine already' (350); the blood of Lucy and Mina circulates within his own bodily economy already, and through the former he has gained access to the transfused fluids of all but Harker. Mina's son, who commemorates the triumphant vampire hunters in 'His bundle of names' (420), also involuntarily commemorates the unacknowledged Dracula, in that she herself has ingested that blood, with its intermingled human and vampire content. The racial and degenerate politics of *Dracula*, therefore, are far from resolved by the vampire's death, for all the superficial containment achieved through the Count's dissolution.[28] The potential heritage of degeneration and miscegenation, it would seem, need not be written clearly on the surface of the body, for all the insistence of the earlier part of the novel.

THE 'SEDUCTION' OF JONATHAN HARKER

In the third chapter of *Dracula*, Jonathan Harker falls asleep in a deserted chamber of his host's castle, shortly after recording the day's events in his journal 'at a little oak table where in old times possibly some fair lady sat to pen, with much thought and many blushes, her ill-spelt love letter' (77). The diary is typical of the man: 'It is nineteenth century up-to-date with a vengeance' (77), he reassures himself, and like his Kodak (64), the shorthand allows him to record dense detail at speed and in a supposedly detached and factual manner. His act of writing is grounded in the 'bare, meagre facts, verified by books and figures' (71) demanded by rationality and secular empiricism. The impossible, in other words, cannot happen; so, when it *appears* to happen – such as when the Count casts no reflection in Harker's shaving mirror (66–7), or descends the vertiginous castle wall '*face down*' (75) – it raises a sense of unease that is inadequately expressed in Harker's suggestion that such things are merely 'startling' (67) or a source of 'repulsion and terror' (75). In Harker's act of witnessing, there is a resistance to impossibilities: under the greatest stress, though, this resistance degenerates merely into a passive refusal to contemplate the danger he currently faces. As Harker says, after witnessing the Count's descent, 'I am encompassed about by terrors *I dare not think of* (76, my italics).

Harker's sense of identity, which is variously British, Protestant, Victorian and Western, is progressively undermined by successive incidents which challenge his world-view. His experiences in the deserted chamber represent but one of these challenges – albeit a particularly personal one, given that his own morality is seemingly tested as much as his grasp of reality. Harker recalls the event:

I was not alone. The room was the same, unchanged in any way since I came into it; I could see along the floor, in the brilliant moonlight, my own footsteps marked where I had disturbed the long accumulation of dust. In the moonlight opposite me were three young women, ladies by their dress and manner. I thought at the time that I must be dreaming when I saw them, for, though the moonlight was behind them, they threw no shadow on the floor. (78)

This encounter is as uncanny and as impossible as the earlier incident of the shaving mirror, to which it is arguably intimate. The absence of a shadow recalls the Count's lack of a reflection (66–7), though a shadow is a transient thing: other than in photography, it leaves no lasting image, no trace that might serve the place of a document. A shadow is not a piece of evidence. What is crucial in Harker's recollection is that 'The room was the same, unchanged in any way since I came into it': the accumulated dust, in other words, has not been disturbed by the entry of the three women, and Harker's own footprints from the door to his couch are evidence that he is the only person corporeally within the chamber. He may explain this impossibility only by claiming that it is the delusion of a dream, as he does both during the encounter, and earlier in the preface to his recollection, when he suggests that 'I must have fallen asleep' (78). Faced with another incident he 'dare not think of' (76), but which his training compels him to record, Harker deploys the dream as a strategy for mental self-preservation. If the encounter *is* a dream, then Harker's world-view, which significantly underpins his identity as a rational, Protestant Westerner, may persist; if it is not, then his intellectual as well as physical self is undoubtedly in peril.

The sense of unease, a consequence of ambiguous evidence, persists beyond the night-time encounter. As Harker notes,

> I awoke in my own bed. If it be that I had not dreamt, the Count must have carried me here. I tried to satisfy myself on the subject, but could not arrive at any unquestionable result. To be sure, there were certain small evidences, such as that my clothes were folded and laid by in a manner which was not my habit. My watch was still unwound, and I am rigorously accustomed to wind it the last thing before going to bed, and many such details. But these things are no proof, for they may have been evidences that my mind was not as usual, and, from some cause or another, I had certainly been much upset. I must watch for proof. (81)

Harker is contemplating his own mental deterioration here at the very moment he seeks to prevent it through recourse to the dream as explanation. He is seeking a certainty which would 'prove' the impossible – and, indeed, seems already half-convinced, as he concludes his journal entry with the recollection of 'those awful women, who were – who *are* – waiting to suck my blood' (81, original italics). It is Harker's two unequivocally wakeful sightings of the vampire, where the Count is first perceived as being 'dead or asleep' (89) and is then found 'looking as if his youth had been half renewed' (92), that confirm the reality of a situation that cannot be a reality under existing laws of thought: his daylight sighting of the 'three terrible women' is hardly so graphic, even if they are depicted 'as licking their lips' (91) in anticipation.

This series of incidents, in which the finality of death is questioned, and the relative value of superstition over rationality upheld, is the cause of the solicitor's 'violent brain fever' (143), a form of nervous breakdown, which Sister Agatha reports in her letter to Harker's fiancée.[29] 'He has had some fearful shock' (143), Sister Agatha informs Mina, and only the most abstruse of readers will conclude that that shock is associated solely with the erotic demeanour adopted by the vampiric trio after Harker becomes aware of their presence. For all that, though, criticism has tended to ignore both the role of evidence and intellectual stress in Harker's collapse into a state which he considers to be a form of madness (148).[30] The emphasis has customarily been upon the vampire women and the sexuality their vampirism apparently encodes. Their identity, though, their place within the lineage and hierarchy of the castle, is in itself worthy of scrutiny.

Harker's recollection of the women provokes a number of potential issues relevant to both the precedent established by Gothic genre, and the twentieth-century interpretation of that precedent by way of psychoanalysis. His account continues:

> They came close to me, and looked at me for some time, and then whispered together. Two were dark, and had high aquiline noses, like the Count, and great dark, piercing eyes, that seemed to be almost red when contrasted with the pale yellow moon. The other was fair, as fair as can be, with great wavy masses of golden hair and eyes like pale sapphires. I seemed somehow to know her face, and to know it in connection with some dreamy fear, but I could not recollect at the moment how or where. All three had brilliant white teeth that shone like pearls against the ruby of their voluptuous lips. There was something about them that made me uneasy, some longing and at the same time some deadly fear. I felt in my heart a wicked, burning desire that they would kiss me with those red lips. (79)

A question immediately arises as to the identity of the three women. Up to this point, Harker has been convinced that he and the Count constitute the castle's sole occupants, his host discreetly undertaking the menial tasks that would normally be done by a manservant (68). The trio have too often and too glibly been styled as 'brides of Dracula', an association no doubt reinforced by the 1960 Hammer horror film of the same title. They are not so called in Stoker's novel: they are simply 'those awful women' (95) for Harker, and for Van Helsing 'the sisters' (412), a term which they themselves adopt when attempting to draw the partially vampirized Mina into their number (409).

The explicitly aquiline features of the first two women might indicate, through physiognomy, a nature as savage and degenerate as that of the Count. It may equally, though, suggest a familial relationship, a shared lineage based upon mortal bloodlines rather than vampiric initiation. The potential closeness of vampire and victim is emphasized in *Dracula*. Arthur Holmwood is momentarily swayed by the sexualized invitation of his un-dead fiancée, Lucy Westenra, in the Hampstead churchyard (255–6), and Harker recognizes that, historically, 'the holiest love was the recruiting sergeant for their ghastly ranks' (341). That 'holiest love', for Harker, is undoubtedly marriage. The close resemblance between the two female vampires and the Count (who becomes 'dark' each time he replenishes his store of blood), however, suggests that they are not wives but daughters, his own offspring. The Count is thus apparently a filicide, one who kills his own descendents, and has become so simply to feed his own perverse appetite, condemning the souls of his own flesh and blood to eternal 'paths of flame' (250) as carelessly as he later does that of Lucy Westenra.

If one equates vampirism with sexual activity – as Arthur seemingly does when encountering Lucy in the churchyard, and as academic criticism has characteristically done in the twentieth and twenty-first centuries – the implications of this familial relationship become even more problematic. If it is possible to term the women 'brides' because vampirism and sexuality are closely related, then the Count is not merely a polygamist but is engaged in incest also. Incest is an established theme in Gothic.[31] It is one of the implications of Manfred's attempt to marry his son's bride in *The Castle of Otranto* (1764), the first Gothic novel, and is rendered both explicitly and graphically in the rapacious activities of Ambrosio in Matthew Lewis's *The Monk* (1796). Its currency has continued into modern Gothic, and one might note here, for example, the ambiguous relationship between Lestat and his mother in Anne Rice's *The Vampire Lestat* (1985), or the seduction of Wallace Creech by his vampire-obsessed daughter Jessy in Poppy Z. Brite's *Lost Souls* (1992).

The potential of the Count's implicit incest was first explicitly acknowledged not in literary criticism, but in *Mark of the Vampire*, a cinematic adaptation of Stoker's novel released in 1935. This MGM film, directed by Tod Browning and starring Bela Lugosi as Count Mora, was essentially a development of Stoker's work, albeit without the sanction of Stoker's widow and Universal Studios, the stakeholders in the *Dracula* copyright. Carol Borland, who played the vampire's dark-haired, equally vampiric daughter, Luna, suggested that 'there was never any question that Lugosi was replaying his famous Dracula part', his definitive performance in the 1931 Universal *Dracula*. She was equally clear as to the original intentions of a script somewhat tamed by interwar censorship:

> in the film, Lugosi's Count appears with a bullet hole in his forehead, which is never fully explained. Well, according to the original script the Count had committed a terrible sin which had lost him his chance of peace after death. He had committed incest with Luna, then strangled her and shot himself.[32]

Mark of the Vampire is, of course, not Stoker's *Dracula*, but it is, in a sense, a type of commentary. Its foregrounding of the incest motif reflects the growing influence of psychoanalysis in the interwar years, an influence which was to shape the earlier years of *Dracula* criticism. In both *Mark of the Vampire* and subsequent critical commentary, incest is no longer merely a Romantic or a Gothic preoccupation. It gains a psychological as well as a generic significance, and invokes associations of repression and guilt. Those associations, inevitably, affect not merely the Count's relationship to the women, but also Harker's own simultaneous feelings of attraction and repulsion. Indeed, at times they further enforce an identity between the fictional solicitor and the author himself.

Twentieth-century psychoanalytical criticism has argued that the two darker 'sisters' represent figures from Stoker's own, sexually tormented, past. Daniel Lapin, for example, in a study which alleges that Stoker's father routinely sexually abused his children, states that these two 'are either Dracula's *daughters*, in which case they would have to derive unconsciously from older sisters (viz. father's daughters), or, more likely, they are Dracula's *sisters*, in which case they derive unconsciously from father's sisters, Bram's aunts'.[33] In Lapin's analysis, Harker-as-Stoker cannot escape the clutches of repressed memory or unacceptable, incestuous desire. Either he sees (and desires) the daughters whom his father already possesses, or else he is erotically menaced by two older relatives, again sexually compromised by the attentions of their male sibling.

The blonde woman represents a psychological problem in her own right, given that Harker 'seemed somehow to know her face, and to know it in connection with some dreamy fear' (79) which he is unable to remember. Phyllis Roth notes that 'Critics have speculated that this fair woman is especially frightening to Harker because she resembles Lucy Westenra, Harker's mother, or simply a typical English girl.'[34] There is no evidence in the novel, though, that Harker has ever met Lucy, who has been a finishing-school pupil of his fiancée. The complexion of the solicitor's mother is also obscure – his employer, 'who treated him like his own son' (201), appearing to be the only parental figure in the lives of both Harker and his orphaned wife (200–1). Roth is tantalizingly vague, too, as to *how* this character may suggest an English prototype.

A mother, though, may have a psychological significance which exceeds the specific boundaries of fictional characterization. Daniel Lapin, in common with earlier critics, regards Harker's uneasy recollection as a tacit acknowledgement that the fair vampire 'is/was the Count's wife, and may therefore be understood as a mother derivative'.[35] In Lapin's study, the Count has strong associations with Stoker's father: hence, in *Dracula*, the prototypically Oedipal desires of both character and author are brought together, the son wishing to dispossess the father of the desired mother, or the vampire of any number of desired women.

Though Lapin does not make the connection, one might perceive here also an anticipation of Mina's later sexual location between the Count and her husband: she is, notably, a woman who, 'mothers' Harker through an illness which kept him as bedridden as the youthful Bram Stoker. She is an object of nurturance and desire, taken from the young male by the older father-surrogate. In this psychological sense, it makes little difference that the vampire is fair and Mina dark. The novel, in this respect, re-enacts a scenario of desire, loss and attempted reassimilation with the object of desire several times. It is small wonder, given the competing forces of desire and guilt that Harker's encounter with the three vampires is conveyed in increasingly ambivalent language, for there is always 'a bitter underlying the sweet' (79).

These alternating emotions add to the sense of confusion which permeates Harker's account. He himself desires, and yet is the passive object of another's, more assertive, desire. Lying down, he assumes the female position in missionary intercourse, for, as Christopher Craft argues, in this encounter Harker apparently 'enjoys a "feminine" passivity and awaits a delicious penetration from a woman whose demonism is figured as the power to penetrate'.[36] Indeed, the analogy is such that Harker is scripted as a virgin, fearful yet sexually aroused, awaiting defloration by a more experienced lover, for the blonde vampire is told by her fellows that 'Yours is the right to begin' (79).

The words and demeanour of the three vampires, as mediated and interpreted by Harker, *should* lead him to conclude that their intentions are conventionally sexual rather than vampiric. The focus, though, is emphatically oral rather than genital. When the blonde vampire states that 'He is young and strong; there are kisses for us all' (79), her meaning encodes both a sexual and an occult meaning. The kiss is a common component of sexual foreplay, and much of Harker's subsequent account reads like a tantalizingly deferred consummation, 'an agony of delightful anticipation' (79) that is never satisfactorily concluded. Harker recalls how:

> The girl went on her knees, and bent over me, simply gloating. There was a deliberate voluptuousness which was both thrilling and repulsive, and as she arched her neck she actually licked her lips like an animal, till I could see in the moonlight the moisture shining on the scarlet lips and on the red tongue as it lapped the white sharp teeth. Lower and lower went her head as the lips went below the range of my mouth and chin and seemed to fasten on my throat. Then she paused, and I could hear the churning sound of her tongue as it licked her teeth and lips, and I could feel the hot breath on my neck . . . I could feel the soft shivering touch of the lips on the super-sensitive skin of my throat, and the hard dents of two sharp teeth, just touching and pausing there. I closed my eyes in languorous ecstasy and waited – waited with beating heart. (79–80)

If the kiss itself never quite happens, then the act of penetration, sexual or vampiric, is similarly deferred. The kiss, in its move from the face down to the lower regions of the body recalls, without actually mentioning them, a series of culturally taboo and non-reproductive sexualities centred upon oral-genital contact. Harker may as well be anticipating an act of fellatio as much as one of penetrative intercourse: this, certainly, is how the scene is interpreted in Francis Ford Coppola's 1992 cinematic adaptation, *Bram Stoker's Dracula*. It should be remembered, however, that in *Dracula* the kiss will always suggest the literal bite of the vampire. The oral and the genital combine in a bite which is both penetrative and associated with sucking; similar conflations and confusions, psychological and consciously symbolic, are associated with the mouth and vagina, and the teeth and penis.

If Harker is perturbed by his anticipation of a taboo oral-genital contact, then he should be similarly shaken by what is for him an unprecedented display of overt female sexuality. Critics, as John Allen Stevenson argues, have concurred that 'Stoker is expressing what have usually been regarded as typical Victorian attitudes about female sexuality' in this portrayal of the vampiric trio and, indeed, in subsequent depictions of the vampirized figures of Lucy and Mina.[37] Under this critical gaze, the prototypical and idealized Victorian woman was sexually modest, if she were considered to have a sexuality at all. Overt female sexualities were the preserve of prostitutes, the promiscuous working classes, and foreign races. Again, it might be suggested that for a woman to *become* openly sexual is for her to become foreign. After the Count's departure, Harker realizes that he is 'alone in the castle with those awful women', though he reassures himself that 'Mina is a woman, and there is naught in common' (94). This is a shallow reassurance, however: the Count's female associates, one must assume, were once mortals such as Mina. So, as Gail Griffin suggests, 'the worst horror' that both Harker and his culture can imagine is not the Count himself but 'the released, transforming sexuality of the Good Woman', and the associated fear 'that at heart, the girls they all love are potential vampires, that their angels are, in fact, whores'.[38]

Harker's encounter with the three vampires thus suggests the dissolution of customary and accepted gender boundaries as much as it does the presence of sexual taboos ranging from premarital sexuality to oral-genital contact. The implications exceed their sexual focus in the novel: where Stevenson sees in Harker's passivity 'A swooning desire for an overwhelming penetration', Victor Sage projects a considerably more far-reaching 'atavistic swoon', an 'abnegation of the will' in which Harker first mentally, and later physically, degenerates as a consequence of his intimacy with the Count and his minions.[39] Progressively, the solicitor loses his rationality and his detachment, his Britishness and his faith in stable gender and sexual boundaries. The vampire seeks to absorb his very being, and if this is not achieved through the supernatural ingestion of blood then it becomes a matter of a more prosaic appropriation of personal property and appearance. The Count actually *becomes* Harker for a while, dictating the content of his letters (82) and dressing in his clothes (85). Without his 'letter of credit' (84) and the other papers which confirm his status as a Western traveller abroad, Harker is no one, has no nation, is (to recall the Count's own words) 'a stranger in a strange land' (61). He has become a version of the degenerate that is the Count. The boundaries of east and west, of employer and employee, of living and dead, and of technology, religion and superstition, break down for Harker at the same time as the demarcations associated with gender: it is little wonder that Harker's explanations to the nuns at Budapest are depicted as 'the ravings of the sick' (147). They represent not merely Harker's disturbed mind but also the potential of a degenerate society which is itself 'sick', where men are weak and women assertive, and even the absolute of Death can no longer be relied upon.

Harker's reverie is abruptly terminated by the arrival of the Count, whose 'wrath and fury' exceeds even the 'rage' and 'passion' displayed by the thwarted blonde vampire (80). Though the Count's angry demeanour projects a male assertiveness and physical presence considerably in excess of that exhibited by the trio of women – he forces them back with 'the same imperious gesture . . . used to the wolves' (80) earlier in the novel (54) – it is his words to them which have attracted the attention of modern criticism. Forcing them back, he exclaims 'How dare you touch him, any of you? How dare you cast eyes on him when I had forbidden it? Back, I tell you all! This man belongs to me!' (80). The Count's proprietorship arguably has a practical basis: Harker needs to be kept alive so that the vampire may complete all the legal formalities associated with his purchase, and may gain also further experience in English diction and culture. However, the somewhat intense relationship that the Count has enjoyed with his guest – freely entering his bedroom (66), making his bed (68), undressing him (81) and wearing his clothes (85, 89) – suggest what Talia Shaffer calls an 'intimacy, acquaintance with the contours of each other's bodies, ease with the prospect of each other's nakedness'.[40] There is thus a further sexual and cultural taboo that may be encoded into vampirism – that of male homosexuality.

As Christopher Craft argues, the presence of the female vampires cannot dissipate the homosexual threat that stems from the Count:

> we must remember that the vampire mouth is first of all Dracula's mouth, and that all subsequent versions of it (in *Dracula* all vampires other than the Count are female) merely repeat as diminished simulacra the desire of the Great Original . . . This should remind us that the novel's opening anxiety, its first articulation of the vampiric threat, derives from Dracula's hovering interest in Jonathan Harker: the sexual threat that this novel first evokes, manipulates, sustains, but never finally represents is that Dracula will seduce, penetrate, drain another male.[41]

If the Count may be read as a predatory homosexual, then two contrasting critical possibilities present themselves, in accordance with the alternating feelings of attraction and repulsion that characterize Harker's response to the three vampires. On the one hand, the novel may express a fear of the homosexual, a dread of being penetrated and made Other by the vampire's contact. Daniel Lapin, again, asserts a psychobiographical context for this component of *Dracula*, with Harker mobilizing the author's own unspeakable fears:

> The three lamiai never actually draw blood, for the Count intervenes, claiming Jonathan for himself. Then Jonathan escapes Castle Dracula before the Count ever actually sucks his blood. Technically speaking, Jonathan was never vamped. It would be foolish, however, to insist that Bram as a child, was as fortunate as Jonathan, especially since . . . the *impact* on Jonathan was clearly traumatic. (original italics)[42]

Fear, though, is equally central to the alternative reading, which associates the homo-erotic script of *Dracula* with the expression of desire for, or attraction towards, the homosexual Count and his ways. The precarious legal and social position of homosexual men in late-Victorian Britain was exemplified in the trials and imprisonment of Stoker's Dublin associate, Oscar Wilde – a former suitor of

Florence Stoker. The year of Wilde's downfall, 1895, was the year in which Stoker is believed to have begun work on *Dracula* in earnest, and, as Nina Auerbach suggests, it might therefore be reasonable to argue that 'Dracula's primary progenitor' is not a fictional vampire such as 'Lord Ruthven, Varney, or Carmilla, but Oscar Wilde in the dock'.[43] For Talia Shaffer, however, the situation is considerably more complex and the text's embodiment of Wilde more ambivalent. Both Wilde and the Count are as perceptibly attractive as they are demonic (or demonized). The vampire, equally, is as much a victim and a prisoner as the young man he holds in thrall. In consequence, the boundaries between the Count and Harker, and between Stoker and Wilde appear to be perceptibly softened in Shaffer's reading of *Dracula* – and the easy equations which may tie Wilde to the vampire and Stoker to the solicitor become less discrete. Developing Auerbach's identification of the vampire and Wilde, Shaffer argues that the Count

represents not so much Oscar Wilde as the complex of fears, desires, secrecies, repressions and punishments that Wilde's name evoked in 1895. Dracula is Wilde-as-threat, a complex cultural construction not to be confused with the historical individual Oscar Wilde. Dracula represents the ghoulishly inflated vision of Wilde produced by Wilde's prosecutors; the corrupting, evil, secretive, manipulative, magnetic devourer of innocent boys. Furthermore, Dracula also carries the weight of Stoker's imaginative identification with Wilde. For Stoker writes Dracula's plot to allow his surrogate Harker to experience imprisonment, just as Wilde languished in gaol. Thus Stoker manages to speak both from the closet and from the open; he simultaneously explores Wilde-as-monster, and identifies with the real Wilde's pain. He writes as a man victimized by Wilde's trial, and yet as a man who sympathizes with Wilde's victimization.[44]

Hence, there are 'codes for the closet' in *Dracula*.[45] The private, gay Stoker admires and even desires Wilde; the public, heterosexual author and theatrical personality is obliged to condemn Wilde's sin – if only by not mentioning his name in his biographical reminiscences. *Dracula* thus becomes a necessary evolution of how a closeted gay man might express his ambivalence towards his own sexuality in the difficult times after the Wilde trial: the novel becomes a further strategy in the author's life of concealment and coding, one of many 'carefully elaborated mechanisms through which Stoker routed his desires'.[46] The three female vampires are thus *just* sufficient to dissipate an unequivocally homo-erotic interpretation of the novel's vampirism – even though the Count's insistence that 'This man belongs to me!' (80) appears to suggest the very opposite. The most striking feature of the Count's obvious interest in Harker is that he does *not* touch him in that most intimate of ways – the kiss, which is symbolically the bite, the penetration, the mixing of bodily fluids. Had the Count done so, Harker would have found himself in the same position in which his wife later perceives herself to be, 'unclean', excluded, shameful, condemned in God's eyes (340). Harker's escape from the castle, desperate and debilitating though it may be, signals not merely his rejection of the unacceptable sexuality which the vampire emblematizes, but also a change in his own identity. He has, as it were, ceased to identify with the passive medieval maiden whose writing desk he has appropriated (78), and with the prone figure of the virgin awaiting sexual initiation (78–9). His final words in the castle section of his diary are a call to action, a statement that he is ready to prove a new-found, resolute manliness which may stand up against the heterosexual allure of the female vampires and the homo-erotic threat of the Count. Contemplating both a vertiginous descent and possible death, he states 'the precipice is steep and high. At its foot a man may sleep – as a man' (94).

THE 'DEATH' OF LUCY WESTENRA

According to Carol Senf, the three female vampires which menace Jonathan Harker 'are important primarily to introduce values and beliefs that *Dracula* will explore more fully in Lucy Westenra and Mina Harker, English women who are also infected by the vampire taint'.[47] Senf's assertion is essentially correct, though it does require some further qualification, given the differing backgrounds and experiences of the two heroines. Mina and Lucy do not present the same implications when they display the consequences of the vampire's bite. They represent differing, possibly contrasting, versions of how nineteenth-century culture constructed women as sexual, social and moral beings. The affinity – or hostility – which each feels for the Count and the vampiric lifestyle may be seen as an index of these cultural conventions.

In the case of Mina Harker, the Count's bite (and her subsequent ingestion of his blood) seems to *add* something to her character that was not previously evidenced by her behaviour. Mina's morals, if anything, are arguably more rigid, more constantly under the scrutiny of a vigilant self, than even those of her fiancé/husband.[48] She is, notably, somewhat embarrassed by Jonathan's public display of affection and proprietorship in Piccadilly, though she excuses herself by saying that 'you can't go on for some years teaching etiquette and decorum to other girls without the pedantry of it biting into yourself a bit' (215). Jonathan's taking of Mina's arm is hardly the 'very improper' (215) act that she interprets it to be, however momentarily: she only accedes to it, it might be argued, because 'it was Jonathan, and he was my husband', though there are suggestions of a more flexible attitude in her courtship days and in situations where 'we didn't know anybody who saw us – and we didn't care if they did' (215). Because Mina's morality is recalled so insistently in the novel, the 'so bright eyes' (406) that she exhibits to Van Helsing in Transylvania are, without doubt, shocking. They are the eyes of vampiric hunger rather than of delicate reserve, and they retain an inevitable association with awakened or active sexuality – a sexuality rendered implicitly in Stoker's novel, though more emphatically in the corresponding scene of Coppola's *Bram Stoker's Dracula.*[49]

Throughout Mina's period of collusion with the Count, the Van Helsing circle is insistent that vampirism – and thus the sexuality associated with the vampiric state – is an imposition upon a woman who, the professor insists, is from the start 'So true, so sweet, so noble, so little an egoist' (232). 'Madam Mina, our poor, dear Madam Mina is *changing*', Van Helsing states, and he 'can see the characteristics of the vampire *coming* in her face' (366, my italics). The whole group is aware that, once vampirized, 'so far as symbols went, she with all her goodness and purity and faith, was outcast from God' (351). The stress on 'symbols' here is crucial. Mina's 'outcast' or Othered status is signified not by her own innate physiognomy, as is the case with the Count, but by facial features *added* to her physiognomy, and a stain *imposed* upon her forehead (339–40). When Van Helsing concedes that Mina may 'have to *bear* that mark until God himself see fit' (340, my italics), he stresses again that the mark is burden, an addition which she must carry: it is not part of her. With the death of the Count, the stain is taken off, the burden is lifted and has 'passed away' (420) as Quincey Morris remarks. It, and what it stands for, has gone beyond her, become separate once more, implicitly leaving behind a Mina whose integrity may no longer be questioned.

Mina's purity is such that the Count can be interested in her only for her strategic value, her insight into the world of his pursuers and her potential as a disruptive presence in their campaign. She herself realizes this, and explains how, by his command, her 'true' (232) nature might be eclipsed 'by wile, by any device to hoodwink – even Jonathan' (370). There is, however, no indication of a sensuality on her part that might be aligned with the Count's own desire, no taboo longings that he might appropriate or overwrite into those of vampiric hunger. Really, Mina and the vampire have nothing in common. The Count, however, has a great deal in common with Lucy Westenra. Indeed, their affinity for one another is such that it is reasonable to argue that the Count's first victim on English soil is not so much tainted as liberated.

The nascent signs of the sexualized postures that Lucy will adopt as a vampire are indubitably prefigured in her flirtatious behaviour towards her three marital suitors. Lucy does not simply record their proposals, but rather gloats upon the attention she has received and the effect that she has upon the unsuccessful Seward and Morris in particular. She gleefully records, for example, Seward's visible nervousness, and how 'he almost managed to sit down on his silk hat, which men don't generally do when they are cool' (98), and gently mocks the American slang that precedes Morris's 'perfect torrent of love-making' (100). The three suitors are displayed almost like trophies in her letter to Mina, with 'number One' who 'came just before lunch' (98) followed by 'number Two' who 'came after lunch' (99), the latter provoking, in Lucy, 'a sort of exultation that he [Morris] was number two in one day' (100). Even Arthur Holmwood, the successful suitor, and 'number Three' (101) in her tabulation of the day's events, is presented to Mina in terms of passion rather than romance, his unchaperoned proposal proceeding so rapidly that 'it seemed only a moment from his coming into the room till both his arms were round me, and he was kissing me' (101).

Though Lucy dismisses herself as being, at worst, 'a horrid flirt' (100), critics have rightly drawn attention to the introspective aside embedded within her account of Morris's proposal, and its suggestion of a more assertive sexuality. Lucy writes:

My dear Mina, why are men so noble when we women are so little worthy of them? . . . Why can't they let a girl marry three men, or as many as want her, and save all this trouble? But this is heresy, and I must not say it. (100)

This is a perplexing statement. Its initial sentiments are quite in tune with Stoker's characteristic sexism. Lucy's words betray a textual commitment to the innate superiority of the male over the female, the female voice here taking a stand opposite to that of the late-Victorian feminists whose claims and activities apparently fascinated Stoker as much as her counterpart, 'the "ideal" woman, so unnaturally feminine'.[50] The approved and 'noble' male is chivalric and active: Harker, notably, has to *attain* these things by trial and endurance during and following his time in Dracula's castle, though it would appear that Lucy's suitors, adventurers all (103), already possess them at this juncture.[51] The corresponding female is not merely distanced from the active world of adventure and intellectual endeavour, but is conscious of her secondary nature, her unworthiness and thus her necessary dependence upon the suitor, lover or husband who forms her binary counterpart. Similar scenes of female self-abasement punctuate Stoker's fiction, particularly after *Dracula*, and also inform the later chivalric defence of Mina Harker, a woman who is worthy, but perceived by herself as 'unclean' (340) and deserving of 'pity' (352).[52]

Lucy's subsequent question appears to evoke polygamy or, if 'have' is taken in the sense of 'possession', a euphemism for sexual intercourse, erotic activity with a succession of partners – and vampirism. This, certainly, is how criticism has interpreted Lucy's words. Margot Gayle Backus, for example, suggests that 'Lucy's genesis from nineteen-year-old belle of the London marriage market to "a foul Thing" [258] to be hunted down and destroyed begins . . . with the three marriage proposals . . . and her expressed desire to run afoul of the British system of domestic reproduction'.[53] Elsewhere, Ken Gelder argues that 'Lucy reveals through her letters to Mina that she already has a sexual "appetite" – as if her transformation into a vampire later on simply makes manifest what was privately admitted between friends.'[54] If, as Carol Fry suggests, successive marriage proposals are, in fiction, 'a frequently used method of establishing worth in women', then Lucy's admission represents a serious undermining of her value in the privy eyes of the reader, at least.[55]

Lucy's 'heresy' may thus be as much a matter of offending social convention as it is of challenging biblical prohibition. For all this, though, it may equally function as another indicator of her frivolity. Such a thing cannot conventionally happen, as it were, in a modern Christian country, and so the utterance is arguably not so much a shameful Freudian slip as an indicator of her idle naïveté. What the remark *does* certainly suggest is Lucy's low sense of self-esteem – the more so when taken in the context of her earlier admission of female unworthiness. Her rhetoric, however light-hearted, suggests that her perception of personal value lies not in her own sense of identity, but in the values that her suitors and aspirant lovers impose upon her. Given the idealism of her suitors during this and subsequent scenes, her appeal to them is as much based on an etherealized romanticism as it is upon a more carnal desire.

Once inducted into vampirism, however, Lucy's idle fantasies assume a physical and erotic immediacy that far exceeds their earlier, apparently innocent, expression. This evolution of Lucy's desire, from private speculation to open, public and bodily expression, is conveyed in *Dracula* through a distinctive and recurrent pattern of language that links Seward's recollections of Lucy with a document he has no knowledge of – Harker's account of the three female vampires. The use of strikingly similar language and imagery in both accounts is doubly significant. On the one hand, it corroborates Harker's diary, disarming any residual doubt that may be associated with his admission of a temporary madness (148). On the other, it projects the implications of Lucy's behaviour beyond the bounds of both the novel and fictional vampirism. It should be remembered that the two accounts are founded upon the assumption that the women observed are conventional mortal creatures. If the language of Harker's diary conveys his fear not of vampires but of sexuality generally – and of sexually assertive women specifically – then it is logical to argue that the depictions of Lucy record gestures which Seward has interpreted as sexual rather than vampiric. In effect, a linguistic register, a discourse, is being engaged in both accounts, and the novel has become implicated in language conventionally used to describe not vampirism but sexuality.

Compare, for example, Lucy's behaviour on her deathbed with her un-dead demeanour in the churchyard. In the former case, Seward recalls how

Arthur took her hand and knelt beside her, and she looked her best, with all the soft lines matching the angelic beauty of the eyes.

Then gradually her eyes closed, and she sank to sleep. For a little bit her breast heaved softly, and her breath came and went like a tired child's.

And then insensibly there came the strange change which I had noticed in the night. Her breathing grew stertorous, the mouth opened, and the pale gums, drawn back, made the teeth look longer and sharper than ever. In a sort of sleep-waking, vague, unconscious way she opened her eyes, which were now dull and hard at once, and said in a soft, voluptuous voice, such as I had never heard from her lips:–

'Arthur! Oh my love, I am so glad you have come. Kiss me!' (204)

Note here the contrast between the romantic, almost asexual hand-holding position of Holmwood, and the invitation issued by Lucy. Van Helsing, realizing the nature of the 'kiss' she desires, interferes – and earns the gratitude of Lucy when she has once again 'opened her eyes in all their softness' (204). The voice, though, is a crucial index of her apparent state of mind – or, at least of the state of mind associated with her 'sleep-waking . . . unconscious' identity.

Later, the vampire hunters witness a second attempt on Lucy's part to engage Holmwood in what might be considered an even more explicit sexual embrace. Throwing the infant she has abducted to the ground, an anti-maternal gesture as striking as the Count's entourage's acceptance of 'a half-smothered child' in a 'dreadful bag' (81), Lucy moves towards her fiancé 'with outstretched arms and a wanton smile' (255). Demeanour and voice are now fully in accord, as Seward recalls:

She still advanced, however, and with a languorous, voluptuous grace, said:–

'Come to me, Arthur. Leave these others and come to me. My arms are hungry for you. Come, and we can rest together. Come, my husband, come!' (255–6)

The specific use of 'voluptuous' links these two recollections of Lucy's behaviour with Harker's own fearful vision of the 'voluptuous lips' and 'gloating' (79) predatoriness of the three female vampires. Harker, notably, sinks into a swoon, a vulnerable 'languorous ecstasy' (80), as the vampires approach, and though the term is not applied to Lucy on her deathbed she *is*, after she is vampirized, described as 'languid' or 'languid and tired' (139) by Mina, and is recalled as taking her last meal 'languidly' (203) in Seward's recollection. Clearly, Lucy's languor is not exactly the same as that experienced by Harker, who is not vampirized. Its use by Seward, though, is wholly appropriate, given that it is a medical term customarily deployed to describe both a circulation deprived of blood, and the bodily lassitude associated with blood loss.[56] In *Dracula*, where the presence, absence, purity and corruption of blood are readily associated with changes in character, morality or identity, the languid body represents a self touched – and modified – by the other. In specific medical terms, the bloodless female body carried a further series of implications associated with the moral consequences of menstruation. As Elaine Showalter suggests, 'One theory held that woman's blood lust came from her need to replace lost menstrual blood', so that (in the words of one Victorian gynaecologist) 'just as a vampire sucks the blood of its victims in their sleep, so does the woman vampire suck the life and exhaust the vitality of her male partner'.[57] 'Woman's blood lust' is here equated to sexual lust, and it is notable that, after death, Lucy deploys her erotic allurements as if she were demanding semen from her 'husband', where in reality the substance she wishes to extract from him is blood. As Victor Sage suggests, symbolically 'The pallid woman is the sexually active, sexually exciting one, though she is a moral threat.'[58] The nature of that threat might be perceived in the way in which Harker is 'infected' with 'languorous' (80) desire even where he is still replete with blood. His sexual passivity, as he imagines it, equates to the desire of those more active in slaking their lustful thirsts.

As Victor Sage notes elsewhere, however, in a consideration of the language of Victorian erotic fiction, 'The term "voluptuous" is a technical term, a ubiquitous part of the code of nineteenth-century pornography.'[59] Hence, in scenes in which Lucy is depicted as being explicitly 'voluptuous' in her language or behaviour, there is a conflation of elements within 'the liquid world', a free association between substances such as blood, semen, breast-milk and tears, fluids which are, variously, taboo, abject, intimate and sexually provocative.[60] If Seward's use of 'languorous' is justified because of his professional training, his use of 'voluptuous' deflects him from the medical world's prototypically impersonal attitude to the patient's body. If, as Sage suggests, 'There is no rigid separation in Victorian pornography, especially sado-masochistic pornography, between blood and sperm', then he and his associates have invested far more than their blood in the body they eventually see, corrupted, compromised and demanding, before them in the churchyard.[61]

Lucy's suitors and her consultant physician, Van Helsing, are fully aware of the symbolics of blood in relation to the transfusions they have willingly taken part in. Van Helsing, indeed, depicts the act of transfusion in far from clinical terms, in that its intention is 'to transfer from full veins of one to the empty veins which pine for him' (164). Van Helsing's imperfect English sustains the ambiguity here: 'him', in context, ought to refer to the blood, metaphorically 'desired' by the empty veins, though it may equally suggest the lover, whose absence may make another 'pine'. Morris, later, is acutely aware of the sexual symbolism of putting one's own fluid into the body of another man's fiancée, for he requests of Seward an assurance that 'Arthur was the first, is not that so?' (194–5). Van Helsing, later, laughs at the irony of Arthur's own adoption of the transfusion as a substitute for sexual initiation, saying – in a sentence that recalls Lucy's own wish to marry all three suitors – that 'this so sweet maid is a polyandrist', with a multiplicity of husbands (219). Certainly, they have each momentarily satisfied her languid circulation: 'something like life seemed to come back to poor Lucy's cheeks' (164–5), Seward recalls, even at the point in which he notes how the 'growing pallor' (165) of Arthur marks the discharge of his fluid into her body.

Though criticism has returned again and again to the apparent connection between Lucy's polygamous fantasy, her four transfusions and the singular attempt to drain Holmwood's blood in the churchyard, it has seldom regarded her vampirism as anything more than a further stage in her developing promiscuity. One notable departure from consensus is Nina Auerbach's analysis in *Our Vampires, Ourselves* (1995), which suggests that 'Vampirism in *Dracula* does not challenge marriage . . . it inculcates the restraints of marriage in a reluctant girl.'[62] Auerbach argues that 'Stoker cleaned up more than he degraded', in that Lucy, as a vampire, 'raises the tone of female vampirism by avoiding messy entanglements with mortals, directing her "voluptuous wantonness" to her fiancé alone'.[63] Lucy's words in the churchyard, indeed, translate her fiancé into her husband, even though, strictly speaking, no ceremony has been performed beyond the initial blood transfusion effected between the two. One wonders, though, what invitations were used to lure the children to 'come for a walk' with the 'bloofer lady' (220) and, indeed, whether Lucy would have remained satisfied had she drained Arthur and inducted him into vampirism, creating a rival as much as a companion. The novel itself seems clear that vampirism is as innately promiscuous as unsanctioned sexuality: Harker fears an 'ever-widening circle of semi-demons' who will 'batten on the helpless' (92), and Van Helsing advocates the eradication of the Count, first for the sake of Mina as an individual, 'and then for the sake of humanity' (362). Vampires, it seems, are never satisfied with a single victim.

Lucy's case, in both its vampiric and sexual aspects, is resolved through a series of actions that alternate uneasily between the medical, the sexual and the occult – and, indeed, between the slick professionalism of the nineteenth-century West and the crude superstition of the feudal East. When Van Helsing prepares the tools appropriate to vampiric exorcism 'with his usual methodicalness', Seward immediately recognizes his actions as 'a doctor's preparations for work' (258). Van Helsing's systematic activity adds a meaning to those incongruous implements – soldering equipment, a blowlamp, some surgical knives and, most extraordinary of all, a stake and a hammer (258) – not available to Holmwood and Morris. Invasive surgery was frequently employed as a cure for female sexual desire by the patriarchal medical establishment of the nineteenth century: Seward might as well be preparing for to amputate Lucy's clitoris, a popular cure for female sexual excess, as for an occult ceremony that is both deeply religious and grossly destructive.[64]

In the ritual disposal of Lucy, though, there is a sense of nostalgia for the 'innocent' Lucy of the past, a desire on the part of the men to 'restore' (259) her to the asexual 'sweetness and purity' (261) they perceive as her 'true' state, in their ignorance of her suggestive letter to Mina. Certainly, the act of exorcism itself recalls a type of sympathetic magic more obviously redolent of sexual symbolism than it is of the theological 'paths of flame' (250) to which Lucy's soul is apparently condemned. The sympathetic magic here – a 'sexual' cure for a 'sexual' disorder, a righteous penetration that will counteract her deviant desire to penetrate – reflects also the desire to violate if not the loved woman, then a body that resembles it to perfection. The novel, effectively, evades outrage by transforming Holmwood's frustrated sexuality into enacted violence, and allowing her other suitors the vicarious pleasure of witnessing his definitive conquest of her desire – though Holmwood's solo performance as lover-cum-exorcist does not unequivocally suggest the 'gang rape' that Elaine Showalter perceives in the scene.[65] Seward recalls how Arthur is first granted 'the right to begin' by Van Helsing (259). The exorcism, in consequence, takes on the symbolic significance of a defloration, a *jus primae noctis* for Arthur which restores his 'right' of assertion and possession. Arthur places the stake over the erogenous zone of the female breast, where Seward pruriently observes 'its dint in the white flesh':

Then he struck with all his might.

The thing in the coffin writhed; and a hideous, blood-curdling screech came from the opened red lips. The body shook and quivered and twisted in wild contortions; the sharp white teeth champed together till the lips were cut, and the mouth was smeared with a crimson foam. But Arthur never faltered. He looked like a figure of Thor as his untrembling arm rose and fell, driving deeper and deeper the mercy-bearing stake, whilst the blood from the pierced heart welled and spurted up around it. (260)

As Victor Sage suggests, in this scene 'The pornographic thrill of rape is unmistakable: blood also equals sperm. In a few thrusting phallic strokes he [Holmwood] turns the white woman into the red.'[66] Lucy becomes red this time because her own blood (or the blood she has consumed) is released, rather than because Holmwood puts his own substance into her. The analogy of exorcism with sexual initiation, the bloody breaking of the hymen, substitutes for the equation between transfusion and intercourse here. There is less of contained seduction in this scenario, more of possession – a term that is relevant to Lucy in both its sexual and occult senses. Thus, the phallic stake imposes what Sos Eltis terms 'a reassertion of masculine dominance and sexual aggression'. Holmwood, as it were restores the right of the male to be the superior sexual predator at the same time as he allows his prey a semblance of the pleasure enjoyed by the erotic and dangerous woman, for he apparently 'drives his fiancé [*sic*] into the orgasmic throes of death'.[67] Even though his fluids do not enter her body through the orifice he has forcibly opened up, he himself betrays signs redolent of breathless sexual exhaustion and liquid discharge, the 'great drops of sweat' (260) that he exhibits having a saline content that links them symbolically to the characteristic saltiness of both blood and semen.[68]

Van Helsing's affirmation that the exorcized Lucy is no longer 'the devil's Un-Dead' but is now 'God's true dead, whose soul is with Him!' (261) is important in dissipating any sense of unease associated with the violent and sexually strident act that has just taken place. The 'dual life' (245) that Van Helsing earlier identifies as a unique factor in Lucy's vampirism, is the essential precursor of this postmortem distinction. As Van Helsing states:

> She was bitten by the vampire when she was in a trance, sleep-walking . . . and in trance could he best come to take more blood. In trance she died, and in trance she is Un-Dead, too. So it is that she differ from all other. Usually when the Un-Dead sleep at home . . . their face show what they are, but this so-sweet-that-was when she not Un-Dead she go back to the nothings of the common dead. (245)

Only through a conceit such as this may Arthur simultaneously venerate the purity of his dead fiancée and violate her body with a passion scarcely concealed behind the 'set' face of 'high duty' (260). 'Is this really Lucy's body, or only a demon in her shape?' (258), Holmwood asks of Van Helsing, immediately prior to the exorcism. If the latter, then any passion, lust or sexualized aggression imposed upon that body by him may be effectively excused at the very moment he is able to enact the unfulfilled desires he once harboured towards her no-doubt provocative mortal body. The sleeping Lucy is the Lucy out of control, lacking volition, a 'different' Lucy, for all the striking resemblance. Lucy's essential soul is absent and thus remains inviolate – indeed, by being drawn away from 'paths of flame' (250), it perversely *benefits* from the violent, sexualized treatment meted out to its former physical home, her body. Arthur's sexual violence becomes almost sacramental.

For Arthur and his associates, Lucy's memory thus becomes a thing of cerebral rather than erotic significance. Through Van Helsing's rhetoric as much as through observation, Lucy's now-vampiric body and immortal soul have been successfully configured as being some-how in opposition to each other, so that the lewd behaviour of the former is perceived as being not appropriate to the purity of the latter. There is no suggestion, of course, that at this stage any member of the Van Helsing circle is aware of Lucy's letter to Mina and its poly-gamous implications. Their horror of her seeming moral deterioration is based upon experience, not documentation: the reader, in this sense, may retain a sense of unease regarding Lucy even after her suitors have attained their closure through the exorcism. Lucy's soul is with God, but her memory persists, purified and rarefied, in the minds of her donors or 'lovers': as Victor Sage concludes 'Now she can rot in peace and her spiritual body will rise on Judgement Day.'[69] Certainly, with her head removed and her body decomposing, she will neither physically attract nor attack anyone: she has become truly passive and asexual, idealized and changeless for eternity.

THE CAMPAIGN AGAINST MINA HARKER

In *Dracula*, only the *consequences* of the vampire's attack on Lucy Westenra are presented directly to the reader. The vampiric act itself is seen only from a distance, the Count being for Mina nothing more than an ambiguous, indeterminate presence, 'something dark' that simply 'stood behind the seat where the white figure [of Lucy] shone, and bent over it' (134). Even Lucy herself can recall only some disembodied 'red eyes' (138) and a pattern of 'specks, floating and circling in the draught from the window' (188), dissociated images that hardly suggest a physical presence at all, let alone an invasive threat. In fact, the bite of the vampire is the great non-presence of *Dracula*. In Stoker's novel, vampires – whether these be the Count's female associates, the Count himself or the post-mortem Lucy Westenra – menace their victims within sight of the diarist and the eyewitness, but do their biting away from the gaze of mortal eyes. The protracted and sensual bite of the vampire, keenly observed from close quarters, acutely detailed and explicitly eroticized, is the stuff of cinematic adaptation and post-*Dracula* erotic fiction, rather than of Stoker's novel itself.

Despite superficial appearances, this statement is as applicable to the vampire's attack upon Mina Harker as it is to the earlier predation of Lucy Westenra. The Count's penetration of Mina and the withdrawal of her blood form but a small part of what is a protracted scene redolent with sexual symbolism, an encounter recalled in detail not once but twice – first by an eyewitness located a few metres away, and latterly by the victim herself. For all her central positioning throughout the encounter, Mina's own recollections of the bite itself are minimal and vague to say the least. She recalls no vampiric foreplay, no teasing – the Count simply and purposefully bares her throat.

There is no recollection of the pain – or even of the very instance – of penetration, and no symbolic orgasm at consummation. As Mina recalls, the Count simply 'placed his reeking lips upon my throat!' (331). Her physiological debilitation consequent upon blood loss and the 'half swoon' (331) she experiences have none of the erotic encodings represented elsewhere in the novel through the 'languorous' and the 'voluptuous' (204, 255). The vampire's withdrawal of her blood is recalled merely as 'this horrible thing' (331): for Mina, it initially lacks definition and symbolism, no matter what it might mean to her husband and the males who gather around her. Though violent and arbitrary, it is not unequivocally equated with rape – and it certainly has no clear associations with sensuality or seduction.

It is thus not the actual bite of the vampire, but the actions which he commits after he has consumed Mina's blood, that form the central, symbolic component of the recollections of witness and victim alike. The uneasy alternation between outrage and titillation that characterizes both accounts mask an important textual renegotiation of Mina's status, not merely as a heroine within the novel but also as a representative of late-Victorian womanhood. The patterns of ownership that the scene imposes upon Mina – where the right to utilize her abilities passes from husband to vampire and, finally, back to husband again – overwrite Mina's own sense of independence and self-possession, expressed and enjoyed since her days of spinsterish employment. In essence, Mina moves from the centre of the group – an otherwise male association – to its margins, returns briefly to the centre following the Count's attack upon her, and then definitively abdicates her power at the novel's close. If there *is* a campaign against Mina Harker in *Dracula*, it is not solely conducted by the vampire for his own selfish purposes. Indeed, it is possible to see in the behaviour of Mina's male associates a reluctance to allow her to maintain the freedoms she has effectively attained as an independent spinster and still retained as a young married woman.

Mina's victimization by the Count is a direct consequence of the decision by her male associates to exclude her from both their counsels and the practical pursuit of the vampire. As Van Helsing says, after briefing the group regarding their enemy's strengths and limitations:

And now for you, Madam Mina, this night is the end until all be well. You are too precious to us to have such risk. When we part to-night, you no more must question. We shall tell you all in good time. We are men, and are able to bear; but you must be our star and our hope, and we shall act all the more free that you are not in the danger, such as we are. (286)

In effect, this decision prioritizes Mina's gender above her talents. Because she is female and thus the appropriate recipient of the group's 'chivalrous' (381) devotion, the need to defend her and to be concerned for her welfare seemingly outweighs any advantage to be gained from her ability to accumulate and process information. Shortly before he withdraws Mina from the group, Van Helsing confides his assessment of her to Seward: 'She has man's brain – a brain that a man should have were he much gifted – and a woman's heart' (279). The coda, the final four words, outweigh all that come before. The two components that make up Mina, Van Helsing suggests, are dissonant even when they are admirable. She is not a harmonious or integrated person, but is as much a hybrid as her formerly feminized husband.

Mina's apparently confused gender identity has a correlative in a polemical figure twice referenced in her Whitby diary. Though Mina's two references to the New Woman in *Dracula* are specifically associated in her diary with issues of appetite and the male's prerogative to propose marriage (133), the late-Victorian reader would be well aware that this often demonized proto-feminist figure was at the symbolic forefront of the campaign for female education and professional status.[70] Mina's sexual conservatism, indexed in her sentiments regarding the marriage proposal (133), thus exists in a tense relationship with her apparently more radical aspirations as an educated woman who earns her own modest income as 'an assistant schoolmistress' (94) prior to her marriage. As Sally Ledger argues, the educated woman was polemically viewed as a masculine woman, one whose learning could potentially damage her reproductive capacity, thus thwarting her biological destiny of motherhood.[71] Though Mina presumably resigns her teaching post in order to support her convalescent husband, her post-marital aspirations still locate her far from vocational motherhood: she learns shorthand and typing, because she wishes 'to be useful to Jonathan' (94) as a clerk or typist – posts prototypically favoured by independent, though less wealthy, New Women.[72] Mina represents, in many respects, a compromise between the aspirations of the New Woman and the acceptable behaviour of the non-working wife: as Sally Ledger argues, it may easily be concluded that, through Mina, Stoker was attempting to fictionally 'terminate the career of the sexualised New Woman, and to reinstate in her place a modernised version of the "angel in the house" – in this case, Mina Harker'.[73]

Scaled down from a New Woman to a dutiful and submissive wife, and left at home in the bedroom, Mina is perversely denied the chivalric protection she would have enjoyed had she accompanied the adventurers to the Count's chapel at Carfax. Though the group are aware that their neighbour is a vampire, and Seward – whose guest Mina is – knows that 'The Count has been to [Renfield], and there is some new scheme of terror afoot!' (316), she is left without the protection of garlic or crucifixes, and is stupefied by narcotics provided at her own request (303, 330). Mina's somatic and cultural passivity hastens her capitulation to the vampire in much the same way as Lucy's trance state negates whatever resistance the heiress might innately have. Perversely, had Mina remained a muted incarnation of the New Woman, an integral member of the team rather than one expelled to the margins of its confidence, she may well have been able to recall, or even possibly resist, the Count's first visit.

The Count's actions *after* he has bitten Mina are those observed when the group break into the Harkers' bedchamber. Seward recalls the scene:

> On the bed beside the window lay Jonathan Harker, his face flushed and breathing heavily as though in a stupor. Kneeling on the near edge of the bed facing outward was the white-clad figure of his wife. By her side stood a tall, thin man, clad in black . . . With his left hand he held both Mrs Harker's hands, keeping them away with her arms at full tension; his right hand gripped her by the back of the neck, forcing her face down on his bosom. Her white nightdress was smeared with blood, and a thin stream trickled down the man's bare breast which was shown by his torn-open dress. The attitude of the two had a terrible resemblance to a child forcing a kitten's nose into a saucer of milk to compel it to drink. (325–6)

With its suggestion of both fellatio and the cuckolding of Jonathan Harker, this scene is as teasingly pornographic as the earlier ritual penetration of Lucy.[74] Seward certainly observes with commendable clarity, but it cannot be said that he truly understands the implications of the tableau in front of him. The reader is left to interpret the sexual implications of her posture, of the blood which implicitly stains her mouth, and of the violence with which Mina's assailant imposes his will upon her. Seward, though, does not specifically note that this is not an act of vampirism akin to that inflicted upon Lucy: the reader is therefore left to draw his or her own conclusions from the relative positions of the two participants.

Mina's subsequent recollection of the event should not be regarded as simply a titillating revisitation of the scenario. Rather, Mina's account adds both analysis and significance to Seward's observations, and affirms that her powers of information processing – which have been so dormant that she appears not to have noticed the bite marks left on her during the Count's first visit – are again active in the service of the group. The central image of the heroine drawing blood from the Count's bosom is recalled thus:

You have aided in thwarting me; now you shall come to my call. When my brain says 'Come!' to you, you shall cross land or sea to do my bidding; and to that end this! With that he pulled open his shirt, and with his long sharp nails opened a vein in his breast. When the blood began to spurt out, he took my hands in one of his, holding them tight, and with the other seized my neck and pressed my mouth to the wound, so that I must either suffocate or swallow some of the – Oh, my God! my God! What have I done? What have I done to deserve such a fate, I who have tried to walk in meekness and righteousness all my days. (332)

Mina's account, like Seward's vision of Lucy in the churchyard, appropriates the language of sexuality to explain the process and implications of vampirism because there is no specialist modern language that can cope with the unprecedented concept of the Un-Dead. It must be borne in mind, therefore, that *all* statements regarding vampires in *Dracula* are approximations, linguistic compromises in which conventional language and concepts are adjusted to express phenomena which, accepted wisdom insists, ought not to exist. Superficially, Mina's account seems to further associate her own passive ingestion of the Count's blood with the sexual symbolics that have earlier been used to describe vampiric penetration. Note particularly her reluctance to name the substance she has ingested, an action which enforces the symbolic conflation of blood and semen. When she asks, 'What have I done?', she seemingly already knows the answer – though it is an answer which may actually be wrong, given the approximate nature of the language which the vampire hunters characteristically bring to bear on the actions and implications of vampirism.

More important than Mina's question. 'What have I done?' is Jonathan Harker's earlier cry, 'What does that blood mean?' (327). The sexual interpretation of the encounter between the Count and Mina has, almost inevitably, overwhelmed all other critical possibilities. Blood is, however, considerably more than a symbolic or psychological substitute for semen. It is, as Foucault suggests, *'a reality with a symbolic function'* (original italics), and its potential significations, always present in *Dracula*, gain an additional impetus from this point in the narrative.[75]

Renfield's assessment of the vampirized Mina, for example, represents an easily overlooked interpretation based upon the presumed quality and relative value of blood as *both* a physiological and a symbolic substance. The dying and distracted lunatic appears to contradict himself. With Mina in mind, he confides to Van Helsing that 'I don't care for the pale people; I like them with lots of blood in them, and hers had all seemed to have run out' (324). However, just prior to this statement, Renfield suggests of Mina that on her second visit to him 'she wasn't the same; it was like tea after the teapot had been watered' (324). Renfield's observations relate to the period of the Count's predation upon Mina that preceded her ingestion of his own blood. The 'running out' of her blood is thus seemingly not a simple matter of depletion or absence. The teapot analogy suggests that it has run out to be replaced or supplemented by another liquid, to be diluted by some other substance. Before Mina drinks the vampire's blood in a pretence of fellatio, she has already been compromised by a more subtle insemination, quietly achieved though an osmotic contact with her veins. The teapot analogy further suggests that her compromised blood has become a weaker substance, is now an inferior quality to its own, lost, pure and unadulterated status. She has become compromised not merely through contact with the Count as an individual, but now embodies – albeit in a dilute form – all that his blood and presence may encode: foreignness, racial difference, cultural and political backwardness, the invasive degenerate in individual and social terms.

A valid comparison may be made with the Count's assessment of his own blood, made to Jonathan Harker at the start of the novel. As Harker recalls, the Count boasts: 'What devil or what witch was ever so great as Attila, whose blood is in these veins?' (70). The Count is here deploying an established Western convention which utilizes blood as a device for illustrating familial lineage and descent from admired ancestors. There is no suggestion here that the Count has *literally* vampirized Attila the Hun. Rather, the Count is simply claiming that he is, familiarly and racially, of one substance with Attila, despite the years that separate the fifth-century king from the fifteenth-century warlord. The two notions of blood relationship, vampiric and familial, exist in a tense relationship in the Count's own circulation, and because of his words to Harker. The Western notion of familial integrity, of an identity founded upon a 'pure-blooded' lineage of known ancestors is undermined by the vampiric promiscuity which supplements one's own substance with the blood of others. The two blood relationships, conventional and occult, enjoy the ability to exchange and interchange, to make conflicting statements regarding the identity of the body in which these ancient and contemporary bloods circulate. Attila's blood is thus compromised or diluted within the Count's circulation not so much because of the passage of time and the presence of other, less glorious, ancestors but because the vampire has ingested the undifferentiated bloods of Transylvanian peasants, Russian seamen and a somewhat sickly British heiress. His consumption of the unexceptional bourgeois blood of Mina might thus seem to be the crowning of his descent into mediocrity – the blood of the ancient king resides next to that of the modern schoolmistress. The Count's desire to ingest contemporary English blood might thus suggest a conscious desire on the part of the ancestrally aware Count to improve his current, compromised blood identity, to overwhelm the substance of a backward race with that of the most modern imperial nation on earth. The irony, of course, is that the Count appears to be coming to a nation whose blood and identity are implicitly decadent and degenerate: in *Dracula*, the heroic male blood of characters such as Arthur Holmwood seems insubstantial in the context of the thirsty, ill-spoken working men who seem to be the motive force of 'the crowded streets of your [Harker's] mighty London' (61).

The Count's supplementing of Mina's blood is associated with a more functional purposefulness, however. Though it is described by

Van Helsing as 'the Vampire's baptism of blood' (365, cf. 386), and is signalled by phrases reminiscent of a marriage service (331), the Count's actions strikingly initiate a state of *communion* between vampire and victim. In liturgical terms, this is specifically the ritual ingestion of a substance in order to share in the quality which that substance represents: in Christian worship, this substance would be either the Eucharistic wine or the bread, which represent the blood and body of Christ respectively. One who takes Holy Communion is, conventionally, termed a Communicant – and the linguistic relationship to *communication* is highly relevant in this specific parody of a religious service.[76] Communication is established not with God, but with one who, in an implicitly blasphemous parody of the Deity, defies both death and time and offers an afterlife to his converts.

The fluid which the Count has his unwitting or unwilling followers ingest brings not a spiritual communion, however, but a telepathic one. Van Helsing's use of hypnotism in order to counteract the vampire's telepathic link with Mina is a reminder of another mythical, if not occult, fluid. Though explicitly a follower of the late-nineteenth-century French hypnotist Jean-Martin Charcot, Van Helsing's posturing while hypnotizing Mina recalls the work of the eighteenth-century pseudo-scientist Franz Anton Mesmer, proponent of an early form of hypnotism known popularly as mesmerism or Animal Magnetism.[77] Mesmer suggested that a telepathic link might be maintained between an operator (or mesmerist) and a patient through the passage of an intangible fluid (usually called magnetism or Mesmerine) from the former to the latter.[78] The fluid enabled a reciprocal response: the mesmerist could 'read' the mind or appreciate the sensations of the patient; the patient, in turn, could 'hear' and respond to prompts or commands issued by the operator.[79] By the end of the nineteenth century, Mesmer's fluid theories had been dismissed, and medical practice considered hypnotism, the successor to mesmerism, to be a form of trance induced in the self, though aided by the hypnotist.[80] Though Van Helsing proclaims himself a devotee of the late-Victorian French hypnotist, the Dutchman's technique, and the model of the mind upon which it is based are recognizably those of Mesmer rather than of Charcot and his immediate predecessors.

Charcot's method of inducing hypnotic trance was restrained and simple: the patient was made to concentrate upon a light, was subjected to physical pressure by the operator, or surprised by a loud noise.[81]

Van Helsing, by contrast, employs a technique strongly reminiscent of the earlier mesmerists and their theatrical imitators:

> Looking fixedly at her, he commenced to make passes in front of her, from over the top of her head downward, with each hand in turn. Mina gazed at him fixedly for a few minutes, during which my own heart beat like a trip hammer, for I felt that some crisis was at hand. Gradually her eyes closed, and she sat, stock still; only by the gentle heaving of her bosom could one know that she was still alive. The Professor made a few more passes and then stopped, and I could see that his forehead was covered with great beads of perspiration. (354–5)

Harker's account is punctuated by allusions to Mesmer's practice, from the 'passes' or hand gestures used to induct the trance, to the 'crisis' that recalls the spectacular hysterical collapses associated with earlier mesmerism.[82] Van Helsing's perspiration further enforces the notion of communication being based upon a fluid medium: sweat, like semen, is a saline substance, and the Professor's facial perspiration here recalls the 'great drops of sweat' (260) which Holmwood displayed on his forehead after the staking of Lucy. Both are signifiers not merely of effort, but also of a new intimacy with the patient who is effectively 'operated' (258) upon.

Perversely, though clinical practice had moved on, the superseded techniques of mesmerism remained as potent images in popular, non-clinical culture. Mesmerism certainly still persisted at the end of the century as both a spectacular stage entertainment and a literary convention capable of denoting charlatanry.[83] Popularly, that charlatanry was associated at times with images of sexual predation conducted by unscrupulous mesmerists – and the interface of trance and erotic states in late-Victorian culture was given a new relevance by Charcot's well-publicized work with hysterical women.[84] This complex of significations proves an uneasy association when set against Van Helsing's obvious altruism, though it does recall the Count's 'possession' of, and intimate contact with, Mina. The Count does not mesmerize Mina through passes or gestures, though he *does* fascinate her with a bright light, a 'red eye' (302), in the manner of Charcot's hypnotism. The count's ability to 'read her mind' (382), and her propensity to imitate his actions (387) as well as appreciate his sensations (388–9), all recall a mesmeric rapport – a contact between operator and subject which, in mesmerism, involves a fluid connection.

The final resolution of Mina's compromised status, and of the greater uncertainty generated by the vampire's presence, comes not with the death of the Count, nor with lifting of the stain from the victim's forehead. It is Mina's pregnancy – achieved through her absorption of another (appropriate) fluid through a different (the correct) orifice – that removes all doubt regarding who finally exercises proprietorship over the heroine. Simultaneously, Harker's literal, conventionally sexual 'possession' of Mina, as evidenced by her child, clears the ambiguity surrounding her gendered identity for once and for all. Mina, as the sole female member of the Van Helsing circle at the novel's close, has an immense symbolic importance. Like Lucy Westenra – who, in a sense, may be said to represent a West that is both corruptible and vulnerable to invasion – Mina is a synecdoche, albeit one whose relationship is not merely to race but rather to (British) womanhood. That womanhood, idealized as it is by the men who see Mina as 'that sweet, sweet, good, good woman in all the radiant beauty of her youth and animation' (351) rather than as their equal in organization, observation and strategy, is confirmed through the biological destiny of motherhood. Culturally, a Victorian woman's place is in the home, nurturing life, rather than in the wilds, defending it. Mina's trip to Transylvania is her final adventure, her last moment of sexual ambiguity and, indeed, the point at which she realizes that she does not wish to share the proffered liberation of the vampiric sisterhood (409). Unlike them, and unlike Lucy, the offspring she produces is a conventional baby, not a converted child in the manner of the 'bloofer lady'. The child's arrival signals not merely the Count's departure, but also the final and ultimate affirmation of Harker's virility and manhood. He, too, may be a father, the begetter of an 'ever-widening circle' not of 'semi-demons' (92) but of mortal descendents. Harker's phallic power, indeed, is greater than that of the noble Holmwood, for he both despatches the vampiric seducer and successfully impregnates the vampire's victim in a literal rather than symbolic sense. The 'girls who you all love' (350) are the Count's no longer: their reproductive capabilities, also, are harnessed to a conventional patriarchal purpose. If Mina has now become the unequivocal property of Harker, Lucy has attained a form of currency as an ideal in common memory.

Mina's accession to motherhood further disarms the threat of challenged or dissolved boundaries that has accompanied the Count's progress across England. Mina, as an (albeit muted) representative of modern womanhood gave up her educational work upon marriage to Harker, in order to support her husband in his professional labours. Her professional skills – the shorthand (94), the stenography and typing (95), even the memorizing of train timetables (381) – leave the public, wage-earning domain and enter the domestic world. They appear in the latter but briefly, utilized by Van Helsing and potentially abused by the Count. Motherhood once more consigns those talents to the domestic sphere, taking them away, even, from their earlier deployment in the service of her husband. Her attention is as focused, and in a maternal rather than business-like sense, upon her child as it once was upon her ailing husband in Budapest (150). The two spheres of domestic and professional life, the distinct demarcations between female and male roles, the stable and familiar boundaries beloved of a society so recently under siege by liquid desires and fluid identities, are restored and affirmed in the reassuring tableau of the novel's final moment.

THE ALLIANCE AGAINST COUNT DRACULA

The American critic Christopher Craft is the origin of a rather unfortunate tendency, often repeated without question in *Dracula* criticism, to refer to the predominantly male alliance against the Count as the 'Crew of Light'.[85] This phrase somewhat limits the potential signification of that alliance. It imposes a simplistic binary upon the novel: if they emblematize 'Light', then the Count must be 'Darkness' personified. These terms retain, of course, moral and theological implications in Western, Christian culture: transparency and opacity of motive; knowledge and ignorance; Christ the Light of the World, Satan the Prince of Darkness. As Van Helsing states, demonstrating the potency of the symbolism conventionally invested in light and darkness, the Count's 'power ceases, as does that of all evil things, at the coming of the day' (284). With this tempting binary reasserted sporadically in criticism after Craft, it is hardly surprising that the novel all too often becomes in analysis either simply 'a morality play' or, more specifically, 'a Christian parody' in which 'Everything that Christ is meant to be Dracula either inverts or perverts'.[86] The 'Crew of Light' is seemingly everything that Dracula is not. There is much, however, in the group's construction, and in its relationship to the Count, that is not theological and which, indeed, resists the binaries and clear oppositions that are so glibly thrust upon it in critical writing.

The textual construction of the alliance against Count Dracula is meticulous, the allocation of individual abilities, social origins and national identities being both complementary and richly symbolic. The alliance constitutes not merely a source of Light to oppose and correct the Count's Darkness, but a collective West to counter his individual East: as Van Helsing says, 'We have on our side power of combination, a power denied to the vampire kind' (282). The group's members are, further, altruistic and self-sacrificing (as Quincey Morris demonstrates), where the Count may, according to Van Helsing, 'do only work selfish and therefore small' (382). The Professor's boast that 'We, however, are not selfish, and we believe that God is with us through all this blackness' (386) again illustrates how integrated the symbolism is in *Dracula*. The group is, finally, meritocratic where the Count is arbitrary and autocratic, is ostensibly democratic (in the limited nineteenth-century application of that term) where he is feudal, and is – perhaps most importantly in Stoker's gentlemanly world – explicitly chivalric where the vampire is a renegade from all mortal morality, and most notably from that pertaining to the treatment and idealization of women.

Despite the physical presence of Mina, women are excluded from the group. This exclusion is achieved not merely by the group's refusal to allocate Mina a status consistently equal to her male counterparts, but also through the very rhetoric which reinforces the alliance's identity. In Van Helsing's heroic vision of the campaign, in which chivalric men 'go out as the old knights of the Cross' (363), there is seemingly no place for the women who – characteristically, if Harker is to be believed – 'had sat and sung and lived sweet lives while their gentle breasts were sad for their menfolk away in the midst of remorseless wars' (78). Mina's 'man's brain' (279) does not reside in a warrior's body – though the same might be said of her husband, whose masculinity is rendered questionable by his introspection at the castle, where he sees himself as a stay-at-home lady-diarist rather than a campaigning knight (78).

If Harker attains a form of masculine credibility through his repeated scaling of the vertiginous walls at Castle Dracula (87, 92, 94), by his attempt to disable the Count with his 'trenchant blade' (349) at the Piccadilly mansion, and in his final assault on the vampire in Transylvania (418), he does not enjoy full privileges within the alliance for much of the narrative. Seward may depict the early Harker as the possessor of 'a strong, youthful face full of energy' (344), but that does not in itself qualify the solicitor as a worthy equal to the doctor and his associates – Holmwood, Morris, and his former tutor Van Helsing. Harker is a newcomer, a parvenu, and has had no contact with the Van Helsing circle prior to the Professor's encounter with Mina, who is herself a friend of Holmwood's fiancée rather than of Holmwood himself.

Harker is brought into the group almost by accident, and he effectively functions as a part of Mina's evidence before he is ever regarded as an active participant in the campaign. Moreover, once inducted to the group, his actions are at first rather menial: he gathers data, talks to working-class carriers (304) and snobbish, petty bourgeois estate agents (309). Later, he reports his findings back to the group (310) like an employee – reading his notes in a deferential manner reminiscent of the way in which he had once reported his labours to the Count (64). Harker is not a gentleman-adventurer: he has never, in the words of Morris, 'told yarns by the camp-fire in the prairies; and dressed . . . another's wounds after trying a landing at the Marquesas; and drunk healths on the shore of Titicaca' (103). He cannot boast of his solo adventures in Europe, nor his (mental) injuries, in the casual manner common to Morris and his kind. Harker is a young man, a traveller, a physically fit man, too perhaps – but not an equal of *these* travellers.

Van Helsing, though, *is* their equal, despite his age (which perhaps makes him rightfully 'first among equals', a leader informally acclaimed by the group's acquiescence to his knowledge and experience). The Professor later proves himself a resourceful traveller and an implacable physical opponent even to the seductive female vampires; but his initial introduction to the group comes through Seward's acceptance of his professional standing. One may assume that Seward was educated at one of the many medical schools in Britain and Ireland, and possibly on the Continent also, as the alienist calls the Professor 'my old friend and master' (155). Van Helsing, intriguingly, was a student in London (157), but not necessarily a tutor. Both men will have been admitted to study primarily because of their ability to pay their fees, rather than simply because of aptitude or merit. Their professional association is founded as much upon financial background as on specialist training. Holmwood, as heir to the Godalming title, would likewise almost certainly have studied for a degree, in order to prepare him not merely for the House of Lords and a likely place as local Justice of the Peace, but also to facilitate his ease in educated company. Morris might well not hold a university degree, but he is – in Lucy's assessment – 'really well educated' (99), and his slang appears to be an affectation for her benefit. Seward, Van Helsing, Holmwood and Morris thus enjoy a great deal in common, the shared values of *mens sana in corpore sano*, which Stoker celebrated in his own life, uniting here in their bodily action, mental acuity and altruistic morality.[87]

Harker lacks the assured confidence displayed by the other male members of the alliance, and is far from easy with his developing status as a legal professional, his unexpected rise 'from clerk to master in a few years' (201). Indeed, when Harker corrects himself on his journey to Transylvania he betrays not merely his recent accession to professional status but also how he attained his position as 'a sufficient substitute' (57) for his employer:

Was this a customary incident in the life of a solicitor's clerk sent out to explain the purchase of a London estate to a foreigner? Solicitor's clerk! Mina would not like that. Solicitor – for just before leaving London I got word that my examination was successful; and I am now a full-blown solicitor! (55)

Harker's hesitation draws attention to how he has qualified. He is a solicitor by Articles, one who has trained part-time while working as a clerk, rather than a gentleman who has attended a university or the Inns of Court. Van Helsing, who lists the higher university degrees of 'M.D., D.Ph., D.Lit., etc., etc.,' (156) on his stationery is also, in his own words, 'a lawyer as well as a doctor' (206).[88] One must assume, given the weight of the Professor's academic credibility, that he did not qualify through the Dutch equivalent of Articles. Harker is perhaps more tolerated than accepted, a man who in consequence adopts a deferential manner in the presence of his new-found associates – until, that is, his wife becomes the centre of the renewed campaign.

It should therefore come as no surprise that Harker is, despite his physical presence, rhetorically excluded from an important scene within the novel during which the alliance is effectively given signification and meaning through the lucid interpretation of the lunatic, Renfield. Perversely, Renfield himself attains a temporary admission to the counsels, his 'dignity' claiming 'a habit of equality' (288) – as a sane man, and as a man easy in a cultured and professional world – that Harker has not yet convincingly displayed. Seward introduces the group to each other thus: 'Lord Godalming; Professor Van Helsing; Mr Quincey Morris, of Texas, Mr Renfield' (288). Harker is not even mentioned, even though his subsequent record is emphatic that he was indeed present: he notes that 'We were all, I think, a little upset by the scene with Mr Renfield. When we came away from his room we were silent till we got back to the study' (292). The repeated 'we' locates Harker within the group, almost as a sort of compensation for his earlier rhetorical absence; notably, the solicitor gives the lunatic the honorary title of 'Mr', thus distancing him temporarily from the social disqualification associated with his confinement.

Harker expresses no embarrassment at Seward's omission of his name. It appears evident, though, that Harker lacks status even in the eyes of the lunatic, who does not question, or even acknowledge, the unannounced guest's identity. He is seemingly less worthy of attention than his wife, who the lunatic has previously met and specifically located within the hierarchy of both the asylum and Seward's social circle: he shows 'courtesy and respect' to her, and affirms that she is 'not the girl the doctor wanted to marry' (277). Even in pain and on his deathbed, Renfield deferentially refers to her as 'Mrs Harker' (324). Harker, it seems, is a man without place, possibly even without any apparent function within the alliance, as Renfield's rapid assessment of the group seems to make clear.

The lunatic follows Seward's introduction with a commentary that might well be taken as a key to the group's composition. The handshake which he proffers to each is in itself an affirmation of equality and trust. Renfield begins with Holmwood and remarks:

> Lord Godalming, I had the honour of seconding your father at the Wyndham; I grieve to know, by your holding the title, that he is no more. He was a man loved and honoured by all who knew him; and in his youth was, I have heard, the inventor of a burnt rum punch, much patronised on Derby night. (288)

This is an extraordinary claim on the part of Renfield, a confined lunatic. If he is telling the truth, his social standing has been considerable.

To have seconded an aristocrat for membership of a prestigious London Club indicates a degree of familiarity far beyond casual acquaintance. Renfield was a member of some standing even before Holmwood's father was presumably balloted for: the reference to a landmark in the racing season, the Epsom Derby, also suggests membership of an aristocratic circle, for only through such privilege would knowledge of the Godalming punch become available to him. Renfield is clearly a man of greater social standing than Harker, and may have once have held the respect of men of Seward's own level.

Turning to Morris, he continues:

> Mr Morris, you should be proud of your great state. Its reception into the Union was a precedent which may have far-reaching effects hereafter, when the Pole and the Tropics may hold allegiance to the Stars and Stripes. The power of treaty may yet prove a vast engine of enlargement, when the Monroe Doctrine takes its true place as a political fable. (288)

This is another extraordinary statement, and one made all the more provocative by its almost prophetic tone. Morris becomes a representative not merely of Texas but also of a potential challenger to British might located not in the east but in the west. The Monroe Doctrine, first proclaimed in 1878, bound the United States not to be involved in European affairs, nor to accept European intervention in American domestic issues. Renfield here looks, if not to actual imperialism, then at least to the use of diplomacy as a means to create an influence that might span half the globe. As Franco Moretti argues, such a fear might underlie Stoker's decision to have Morris die in the novel's closing stages. Moretti sees Morris as an equivalent of the vampire, his monopoly capitalism being as alien to British imperial ideals as the Count's feudalism. Thus Morris – always an ambiguous ally in Moretti's judgement – quietly 'enters into competition with Dracula; he would like to replace him in the conquest of the old world. He does not succeed in the novel but he will succeed, in "real" history, a few years afterwards.' Logically, as a potential rival, and 'for the good of Britain . . . Morris must be sacrificed'.[89] It is a glib and easy thing to regard Stoker's attitude to America as being one of indulgent eulogy, with the United States pictured as 'England's firstborn child' and the two nations seamlessly linked by 'the instinct of a common race'.[90] As Moretti and, more recently, Andrew Smith have demonstrated, the author's sentiments may well mask a sense of foreboding.[91] It is almost as if Morris's eventual death represents an occluded desire to both celebrate American heroism and halt the progress of that nation at the most basic level of the individual pioneer-entrepreneur.

Van Helsing is signalled as being different from the other named members of the group by Renfield's refusal to prefix his name with a title. Even Seward, who needs no introduction, receives the title 'Dr' and the specific role of 'humanitarian and medico-jurist' (288). Renfield turns away from familial and national origins, his earlier focuses, in order to praise the Professor's skills as a polymath:

> What shall any man say of his pleasure at meeting Van Helsing? Sir, I make no apology for dropping all forms of conventional prefix. When an individual has revolutionised therapeutics by his discovery of the continuous evolution of brain matter, conventional forms are unfitting, since they would seem to limit him to one of a class. (288)

Van Helsing, of course, is not 'one of a class' – his qualifications and experience embrace not merely formal academic disciplines but also practical jurisprudence and the uneasy interface between theology and folklore. Renfield is silent, though, regarding the Professor's Roman Catholicism, which links Van Helsing with the Catholic east of Harker's travels rather than the Protestant west of Morris. His Dutch origins, though, distance the Professor from both the east and the feudal: the Netherlands was an early mercantile nation and, through the intervention of the Protestant prince William III in the Glorious Revolution, a strong influence upon the British Constitutional Monarchy. Though Renfield does not mention it, the Professor's national origins and intellectual speculations quietly disarm his religious difference. As Clive Leatherdale suggests 'Combining his scientific eminence with his Vatican contacts, Van Helsing has connections with two of the dominant forces of Western culture.'[92] He is, as Victor Sage argues, 'the perfect combination of doctor and priest', treating the body and the soul, the physiological, the psychological and the spiritual.[93] Whether Stoker, an Irish Anglican, was conscious of the implicit sentiments of the novel or not, *Dracula* seems to suggest that the increasingly secular though still Protestant-tempered west might do well to expand its boundaries and embrace those parts of the Roman Catholic Other that may serve a demonstrable purpose. Van Helsing's science is more important than his religion – though, as the novel progresses, it becomes clear that he has integrated one into the other, creating an intellectual hybrid which is capable of comprehending both the predictable and the unprecedented. The climax of Renfield's speech to the group is his appeal to them as representatives of the sane and free world. He concludes:

> You, gentlemen, who by nationality, by heredity, or by the possession of natural gifts, are fitted to hold your respective places in the moving world, I take to witness that I am as sane as at least the majority of men who are in full possession of their liberties. (288)

Clearly, to Renfield, this trio (and the appended Seward, who is also mentioned) represent if not an elite, then a credible cross-section of Western ability and aspiration. They are an alliance of good things: the old and the new, the British and the Continental, the Saxon at home and across the seas, those born into wealth and status and those who have achieved it by study or labour.

There is no place for Harker here, and yet there is seemingly no place for the Count also. For all this, he might well have stood within the group had he not become the focus of their antipathy. Perversely, he shares many of the attributes which Renfield associates with the vampire hunters: he is a man of ancestral lineage and inherited wealth; he has developed himself mentally and strategically, albeit at a slower speed than a living mortal; he has successfully supplemented his occult knowledge with an appreciation of secular technologies and social systems – like Van Helsing, he knows the law; like Holmwood, he may hire a ship; like Morris he may seek to expand his sphere of influence. The Count and the Professor, indeed, share a similar physiognomy (58–9, 225), and both have titles which are sporadically dropped in both the novel and criticism.[94] It should come as no surprise that there is a touch of admiration in Van Helsing's assessment not merely of the Count's campaign but also of his character and potential. As the Professor says of the Count, 'He have done this alone; all alone! from a ruin tomb in a forgotten land. What more may he not do when the greater world of thought is open to him' (364).

Van Helsing's ambivalent appreciation of the Count, the secondary role undertaken by Harker for much of the novel, and the status of Seward, Holmwood and Morris as components of the alliance rather than discrete individuals would seem to suggest that *Dracula* has no single hero. The male figures, throughout, balance their heroism and other laudable qualities with imperfections visible to both reader and characters alike. Harker's lack of self-confidence; Seward's scientific dogmatism; Morris's backwoodsman gaucherie; Holmwood's emotional tearfulness; even Van Helsing's fractured English, remind the reader that success only comes to the alliance because it *is* an alliance, because the sum of the parts exceeds the value of any one of the components taken in isolation. The far-sighted and meticulous Count, Harker suggests, 'would have made a wonderful solicitor' (72): but he is also a man of action, intimately familiar with the human body, knowledgeable regarding the occult, an aristocrat and an imperialist in the making. The two sides balance each other: it is the power of the collective that establishes a final superiority. The fight against the vampire is as much a matter of social and political identities as it is the defence of a theological position. In *Dracula*, symbolically as well as functionally, mortal paths of glory replace eternal 'paths of flame' (250).

DISCUSSION QUESTIONS

Narrative Authority

1. Does the multiple narration of *Dracula* enhance or impair its function as evidence? Would the novel have been more effective if told by a single narrator?
2. Does the novel make any distinction between the value of testimonies provided by female rather than male narrators?
3. Does Stoker's reproduction of dialect mock speakers of nonstandard English, or is it acceptable as 'local colour'?

The Gothic Text

1. Stoker's original contract for *Dracula* specified the novel's title as *The Un-Dead*. Would the original title have been more effective in the marketing of the book in 1897? If so, why?
2. Is *Dracula* a derivative work, merely reproducing established Gothic conventions, or does it represent a new development of the genre, more or less independent of its eighteenth- and earlier nineteenth-century origins?

3. Is it possible for the reader to feel sympathy for the vampire, as both Van Helsing and Mina do, or does his evil preclude such sentiment? You might wish to compare the Count here with Victor Frankenstein, a character who is both hero and villain in Mary Shelley's *Frankenstein* (1818).

Dracula in Criticism

1. Non-psychoanalytical criticism has done much to restore the medical, social and sexual conventions of the fin de siècle to public knowledge. Can Stoker's novel, though, be successfully be read without reference to these contemporary contexts?
2. Has the critical tendency to concentrate upon a limited number of scenes and/or characters in *Dracula* inhibited what might be said about the novel? If so, how?
3. *Dracula* has been considered through psychoanalysis, cultural materialism, gender studies and queer theory. What other theoretical developments may be brought to bear upon Stoker's work? How will this affect the future interpretation of the novel?

CHAPTER 4

CRITICAL RECEPTION AND PUBLISHING HISTORY

REVIEWING *DRACULA* 1897–9

On 26 May 1897, a hard-backed, yellow-jacketed novel of 360 pages was quietly released by the London publishing house of Archibald Constable and Company. The bold colour adopted for its cover and paper dust-jacket may well have been chosen in order to give the novel – and its enigmatic title, *Dracula* – a slightly daring, even provocative, allure. Yellow was, at the end of the nineteenth century, a fashionable colour particularly associated with the artistic *avant garde* and the at-times risqué interface of aestheticism and self-conscious decadence. It was the colour of the corrupting novel in Oscar Wilde's *The Picture of Dorian Gray* (1890) and literally suffused *The Yellow Book* (1894–7), an artistic and literary journal associated in particular with the sexual perversity of Aubrey Beardsley's illustrations. Stoker was familiar with *The Yellow Book*, and may well have been a subscriber: copies were listed within his private library when it was sold off following his death. Yet there is no evidence that the author himself suggested, or even approved, of the cover design for *Dracula*. It may well have been a marketing decision made by his publisher. Deliberately or not, however, in 1897 *Dracula* was initially located within the context of the decadent culture signified by yellow – a context which the reader may all too easily overlook when consulting modern editions whose covers reproduce images from films, or vignettes recalling the novel's plot.[1] Through the signification of its original cover as much as its actual content, the implicit suggestion is that *Dracula* is surely a novel of its time, as bound up in end-of-century unease as Rudyard Kipling's poem 'Recessional' or H. G. Wells's novels *The Time Machine* and *The War of the Worlds*, published in 1897, 1895 and 1898 respectively.

The novel's place within the ambiguous and fearful culture of the 1890s is, however, as problematic, and at times as contradictory, as its contents. *Dracula* is a novel that seemingly proclaims the allure of forbidden pleasures – surrender, sexual ambiguity, superstition and the flight from reason, absorption into the foreign or decadent Other – only to assert their suppression by a worthy and conventional morality. Yet the victory of that morality is never final: the death of the vampire never truly undoes the memory of what has been, of the transgressions that have taken place. This uneasily oscillation between competing states of being and identity, this perceptible divergence between cover and content should surely have provoked at least some comment from contemporary reviewers. Again, the apparent sexual implications of the novel, and its almost strident commentaries upon gender, upon race, empire and nationhood, ought equally to have stimulated some acknowledgement from the periodicals of the day. Yet they did not.

Dracula was not, in 1897, a literary phenomenon of any great magnitude. Though well reviewed, it attracted no great controversy. It was neither an important novel of its time, nor indeed *about* its time. In review, it was never considered an evocation of decadent pleasures, not was it taken as a riposte to unlicensed or deviant desire. Nor, indeed, was it even considered a prophetic vision of the West's imperilled present or uncertain future. If not misunderstood in 1897, *Dracula* was a novel inexplicably underanalysed or simply overlooked. It is almost as if the reviewers of late-Victorian Britain failed to even see what appears to be so obvious to a modern critical establishment. One might even be led to wonder how much meaning has subsequently and arbitrarily been *imposed* upon Stoker's novel, making it an index not merely of Victorian issues but also of the twentieth- and twenty-first centuries' visions of what was important to Stoker and his readership.

One of the likely reasons that *Dracula* was not regarded neither as a serious novel nor as a commentary upon the social, racial or sexual issues of its day was the reputation enjoyed by its author. Stoker's reputation lay in theatrical and social circles rather than strictly literary ones, and he was invariably associated with his celebrity employer, Henry Irving. In his *Daily Telegraph* obituary of Stoker, Hall Caine depicted the Irishman as a 'big, breathless, impetuous hurricane of a man', characterized by his capacity for friendship, 'his energy and his enthusiasm' and 'the big heart' which was 'not entirely exhausted even by its devotion to the great man with whom his name is generally associated'. For Caine, a popular novelist, Stoker was not an author with serious or polemical aspirations. Acknowledging Stoker's celebrated ability as a perceptive, as well as an entertaining, after-dinner speaker, Caine asserts:

> I cannot truly say that this deeper side of the man ever expressed itself in his writings. He took no vain view of his efforts as an author. Frankly, he wrote his books to sell, and except in the case of one of them (his book on Irving), he had no higher aims. But higher aims were there, and the power of realising them had not been denied to him.[2]

Again, the subject matter of *Dracula*, its occult and violent content, seems strangely at odds with the genial hospitality of the writer. As the *Detroit Free Press*'s review of the first US edition – issued by the New York publisher Doubleday & McClure in 1899 – suggests, 'It is almost inconceivable that Bram Stoker wrote *Dracula*':

> Think of him.
> He – a great, shambling, good-natured, overgrown boy – although he is the business manager of Henry Irving and the Lyceum Theater – with a red beard, untrimmed, and a ruddy complexion, tempered somewhat by the wide-open, full blue eyes that gaze so frankly into yours! Why, it is hard enough to imagine Bram Stoker a business man, to say nothing of his possessing an imagination capable of projecting Dracula upon paper.
> But he has done it. And he has done it well.[3]

The tone of this American review is affectionate, even where it is humorously incredulous. Like Caine's obituary, it projects a myth of Stoker that differs from that associated with twentieth-century academic criticism. There is no suggestion of social concern, of sexual guilt, of a need to treat fiction as an outlet for frustrated desire or unspeakable personal or social fears. A less indulgent response, albeit one still premised upon the novel as being nothing more than a simple work of fiction, may be discerned among the earlier British reviews that acknowledged the release of *Dracula* in 1897. Even in the most hostile of these, though, there is an acknowledgement of the novel's compulsive plot and engaging style – even where that praise is given grudgingly in the midst of a disdain for its subject matter and likely readership.

The *Observer*, for example, praises Stoker's ability to maintain reader interest in a complex plot throughout a long novel. However, the reviewer intimates that that interest is arguably as unwilling as it is compulsive in that 'the author's undoubted descriptive powers . . . engender a fascination which *forces* one to read on to the end' (my italics).[4] The *Manchester Guardian* expresses similar sentiments regarding the 'complicated' plot of *Dracula*, when its reviewer contends that 'it says no little for the author's powers *that in spite of its absurdities* the reader can follow the story with interest to the end' (my italics).[5] The phrase 'gruesome' is common to the assessments advanced by both reviewers, and is also implicit in a review printed in the *Bookman* which advises the potential reader that

> A summary of the book would shock and disgust; but we must own that, though here and there in the course of the tale we hurried over things with repulsion, we read nearly the whole thing with rapt attention.

The 'audacity' of Stoker's achievement, as the *Bookman* phrases it, seemingly cannot be denied by any of the reviewers.[6] However, there appears to be a significant consensus that regards *Dracula* as a work characterized by bad taste. As the *Observer* concludes, 'Notwithstanding the merits of the book, it is impossible to congratulate Mr Stoker on his theme, which can but feel to be one quite unworthy of his literary capabilities.'[7]

The antipathy towards *Dracula* expressed by a significant number of reviewers seems to be focused in particular upon the novel's perceived Gothicism. Though the generic label 'Gothic' is never explicitly applied to *Dracula* by late-Victorian reviewers, Stoker's novel – whose characters and events are, arguably, as 'nineteenth century up-to-date with a vengeance' (77) as Harker's shorthand – is insistently coupled with literary works from the past rather than the present. As the reviewer for the *Daily Mail* argues,

> In seeking for a parallel to this weird, powerful, and horrorful story our mind reverts to such tales as 'The Mysteries of Udolpho',

'Frankenstein', 'Wuthering Heights', 'The Fall of the House of Usher', and 'Marjery of Quether'. But 'Dracula' is even more appalling in its gloomy fascination than any one of these.[8]

The use of 'revert' is pointed here. To understand *Dracula*, to find its literary model, one must look to the discarded past rather than the evolving or progressive present. The earliest of the Gothic works cited in the review, Ann Radcliffe's *The Mysteries of Udolpho*, was published in 1794. Mary Shelley's *Frankenstein* appeared in 1818, Edgar Allan Poe's 'Usher' in 1839–40 and Emily Brontë's *Wuthering Heights* in 1847. Only 'Marjery of Quether', a now-forgotten short story by Sabine Baring-Gould, was published close to *Dracula* in 1891.

Even those critics who drew favourable comparisons between Stoker's style and the novels of Wilkie Collins maintain this tendency to associate *Dracula* with the literary past. Collins, who died in 1889, published *The Woman in White* in 1860 and *The Moonstone* in 1868: *Dracula* is thus repeatedly compared in review to works published between 37 and 29 years earlier. Even J. S. Le Fanu, another Irish Gothicist favourably compared in review to Stoker, constitutes a relatively distant figure: Le Fanu's vampire novella 'Carmilla' was published in 1872, 25 years before *Dracula*.[9] Stoker may thus be, according to the *Publishers' Circular*, 'the Edgar Allan Poe of the 'nineties', but he enjoys an inferior status when juxtaposed to living authors of repute.[10] As an otherwise favourable review by the *St James's Gazette* opines, stylistically 'Mr H. G. Wells can give Mr Stoker points', albeit in the context of the short story rather than of the novel.[11]

Stoker's novel is not, however, merely an anachronism in terms of its style and subject matter. It is interpreted, equally, as an overemphatic, even excessive, replication of works that were dismissed as ephemeral or crudely popular in the past. The *Spectator*, for example, opens its review with the opinion that

Bram Stoker gives us the impression – we may be doing him an injustice – of having deliberately laid himself out in *Dracula* to eclipse all previous efforts in the domain of the horrible, – to 'go one better' than Wilkie Collins (whose method of narration he has closely followed), Sheridan Le Fanu, and all the other professors of the flesh-creeping school.[12]

Enthusiasm on the part of the author has seemingly eclipsed any commitment to modern good taste. So, in the words of the *Athenaeum*,

'"Dracula" is highly sensational but it is wanting in the constructive art as well as in the higher literary sense'. Specifically, there are apparently too many 'ingenious and gruesome details' in *Dracula*, and 'Mr Stoker's way of presenting this matter, and still more the matter itself, are of too direct and uncompromising a kind' to be acceptable to the *Athenaeum*'s projected readership. That elite readership would no doubt concur that 'At times Mr Stoker *almost* succeeds in creating the sense of possibility in impossibility' (my italics). It would no doubt, though, never concede that Stoker's work was acceptable as contemporary literature suitable for an educated audience. Disdainfully, the reviewer concludes that Stoker's 'object, assuming it to be ghastliness, is fairly well fulfilled', before decrying the taste of those who might be less critical of *Dracula* with the patronizing suggestion that certain 'Isolated scenes and touches are probably quite uncanny enough to please those for whom they are designed.'[13]

Stoker's reviewers were also frequently disconcerted by the novel's transposition of the Gothic from a medieval or eighteenth-century (and often European) milieu to a modern British setting. The *Manchester Guardian*, for example, follows a cautionary preface with some grudging praise regarding the novel's relocation of 'a medieval noble' to the modern world:

A writer who attempts in the nineteenth century to rehabilitate the ancient legends of the were-wolf and the vampire has set himself a formidable task. Most of the delightful old superstitions of the past have an unhappy way of appearing limp and sickly in the glare of a later day, and in such a story as *Dracula* by Bram Stoker . . . the reader must reluctantly acknowledge that the region for horrors has shifted its ground.[14]

The *Spectator* is less happy to concede even 'reluctant' praise for the intrusion of ancient, feudal European horrors into the technological world of late-Victorian Britain. The review's conclusion effectively undermines the few positive things it said regarding 'Mr Stoker's clever but cadaverous romance', primarily its 'invention of incident' and 'thrilling details', with the uncompromising statement:

Mr Stoker has shown considerable ability in the use that he has made of all the available traditions of vampirology, but we think his story would have been all the more effective if he had chosen an earlier period. The up-to-dateness of the book – the phonograph diaries, typewriters and so on – hardly fits in with the medieval methods which ultimately secure the victory for Count Dracula's foes.[15]

The overall impression that might be gained from the British reviews of 1897 is that *Dracula* is forcefully written, yet is a readable work *despite* its genre and subject matter rather than *because* of them. Part of the problem, for some elite reviewers at least, would appear to be the perceived inappropriateness of the Gothic as a vehicle for the expression of acceptable sentiment and incident at the close of the nineteenth century.

Not all of Stoker's reviewers, however, were hostile to the contemporary Gothic of *Dracula*. The *Pall Mall Gazette*, a sensational journal with a largely popular rather than narrowly elite readership, was somewhat more indulgent of Stoker's generic anachronism – if only because the journal was itself fictionalized as one of the documentary components supporting the novel's plot through the incident of 'The Escaped Wolf' (179). The reviewer comments that, far from being inappropriate, 'the lifelike commonplace' lends conviction to an impossible story:

> A glance at your pipe-rack and evening paper will not save you, for Mr Bram Stoker lays the main scenes of his tale in England and London, right up to date, with the type-writer, the phonograph, the *Pall Mall Gazette*, the Zoo, and all the latest improvements complete. That is the way to make a horror convincing. The mediæval is well enough in its way, but you don't care what sort of bogeys troubled your ancestors all that way back.

Where others are tempered in their praise, the *Pall Mall Gazette* celebrated the fact that 'there is a creep in every dozen pages or so': 'For those who like that, this is a book to revel in. We did it ourselves, and are not ashamed to say so.'[16]

Only one contemporary review make any substantial reference to the focus of so much modern criticism – the sexual implications of vampirism, and their potential effect upon the conventional, monogamous morality of the vampire hunters. The London *Times* appears a surprising vehicle for such perceptive and brave analysis, given its long-standing reputation as a staid upholder of the British establishment. Nonetheless, its reviewer notes that:

> *Dracula* cannot be described as a domestic novel, nor its annals as those of a quiet life. The circumstances described are from the first peculiar. A young solicitor sent for on business by a client in Transylvania goes through some unusual experiences. He finds himself shut up in a half ruined castle with a host who is only seen at night and three beautiful females who have the misfortune to be vampires. Their intentions, which can hardly be described as honourable, are to suck his blood, in order to sustain their own vitality.[17]

The 'honourable intentions' optimistically associated with the male role in Victorian courtship are here imposed upon the occult assertiveness of the female vampires: an analogy is quietly drawn between sexual seduction and vampiric predation, in much the same way as is so often the case in modern academic criticism. Further, the review even suggests the possibility of polygamous sexual relations between the four resident vampires, for

> Count Dracula (the host) is also a vampire, but has grown tired of his compatriots, however young and beautiful, and has a great desire for what may literally be called fresh blood.[18]

The review, seemingly teasingly, exposes the literal here in order to suggest the figurative or symbolic. Certainly, there is a suggestion that those who encounter vampires may inherit the symbolic as well as literal qualities of vampirism. The point is subtly made through an allusion to Shakespeare: 'As Falstaff was not only witty himself but the cause of wit in other people, so a vampire it seems, compels those it has bitten . . . to become after death vampires also'.[19] To be a vampire is to desire a substance that is both symbolic and literal, a point reiterated by the reviewer's concluding insistence that the vampire hunters, the opponents of the Count and all his condition may signify, are 'four resolute and highly-principled persons'.[20] Two, unnamed, members of the Van Helsing circle appear to be excluded from this group, though the implication would seem to be that where 'resolute' qualities are those required for the vanquishing of the desire for 'literal' blood', 'principles' are appropriate for the disarming of the troubling, symbolic aspects of vampirism.

The *Times*' assessment is, almost certainly, the most far-sighted of the contemporary British reviews of Stoker's novel. Only one other review would seem to approach its prescience with regard to how academic criticism would eventually interpret not merely *Dracula* but also the condition of vampirism itself. Reviewing the first American edition of *Dracula*, the *San Francisco Wave* declared that 'When an Englishman or, for that matter, anyone of Anglo-Saxon blood goes into degenerate literature of his own sort, he reveals a horrible kind of degeneracy.'[21] Just as *Dracula*, seemingly, could not have been produced by the 'great, shambling, good-natured' theatre manager according to the *Detroit Free Press*, so it *ought* not to have been written by 'an Englishman [*sic*] who calls himself "Bram Stoker"' – or, indeed, any other Anglo-Saxon, according to the *San Francisco Wave*.[22] The 'degeneracy' identified by the latter reviewer is not based upon Stoker's meticulous portrayal of the Count through the medical logic of Lombroso. It is a degeneracy of morals, of taste, rather than of the racial body – but the rhetorical effect is very much the same. The devil, it seems, is in the detail – as is a clue to the specific focus of the reviewer's distaste:

No detail is too nauseating. In the first seventy pages, there are four cases of deaths caused by the preying of human vampires, one murder, one suicide, one lunatic with homicidal mania and a habit of eating flies, one somnambulist, one shipwreck, extent of fatalities not fully reported, one death by hysterical fright. Pleasant, isn't it?[23]

The protracted and rhetorical tabulation of 'nauseating' detail, together with opening comments which compare *Dracula* unfavourably even to 'The works of the French degenerates', suggest that the reviewer is rhetorically associating Stoker's novel with the French school of naturalistic fiction, popularly typified by the works of Emile Zola and others, rather than with the Gothic tradition favoured by English reviewers. The popular association between French fiction, the portrayal of vice and the decline of public morals is here imposed upon a British work that seemingly opposes the very physical and cultural deteriorations that Zola and his associates meticulously and controversially chronicled. Citing the restrained suggestion of horror in Robert Louis Stevenson's *The Strange Case of Dr Jekyll and Mr Hyde* as representative of the standard which *Dracula* has failed to reach, the reviewer finally concludes that the latter is a 'literary failure' consequent upon a 'lack of artistic restraint' exercised by the author. One can only speculate that the outwardly moral and gentlemanly Stoker might have felt somewhat wounded by this acid assessment, had it been drawn to his attention. It is not certain whether he knew of the review, though he did subscribe to an agency which provided him with press cuttings related to his activities and public appearances.[24] The content of Stoker's late essay, 'The Censorship of Fiction' (1908), however, may well in itself suggest that he was aware of the *San Francisco Wave*'s hostility. His plea in that essay, that authors employ a degree of personal self-control (which Stoker calls 'self-restraint' or 'reticence'), would seem to be directed against the 'lewd subjects' of the 'problem novels' which presumably inflamed the American reviewer in 1899.[25] Stoker could hardly have chosen a more emphatic way to distance himself, and indeed *Dracula*, from the scorn associated with Zola and his imitators, the producers of 'a class of literature so vile that it is actually corrupting the nation'.[26]

THE RISE OF THE CRITICAL EDITION

Dracula appears to have received little – if any – attention from reviewers following the publication of its first British and US editions. Subsequent editions and reprints, if acknowledged at all, usually attracted only a line or two signalling their existence, rather than any comment upon the novel's content. The textual integrity of *Dracula*, interestingly, has remained remarkably stable in the hundred years following its first release. Though Stoker prepared an abbreviated paperback edition for Constable in 1901, the vast majority of subsequent editions have retained the full text of the 1897 original. Constable retained the title on its catalogue until 1920, though cheap mass-market hardbacks were published in the United Kingdom by Rider and Company from as early as 1912, the year of Stoker's death. Rider, an imprint associated with the production of popular occult works as well as supernatural fiction, kept *Dracula* in print until the mid-1950s, before passing the title to Arrow and Jarrolds, who were part of the same publishing group. Arrow kept a paperback edition of *Dracula* in print until 1979, in conjunction with shortened versions of Stoker's

The Jewel of Seven Stars, The Lady of the Shroud and *The Lair of the White Worm*.[27] A similar movement from hardback to mass-market paperback may also be observed in the reprinting of *Dracula* in the United States. The novel was, however, marketed there in connection with a film adaptation – Tod Browning's Universal *Dracula*, starring Bela Lugosi – as early as 1931.[28] This marketing ploy did not reach Britain until 1979, the year of Universal's remake of *Dracula*, starring Frank Langella.[29] Christopher Lee's cinematic portrayal of the Count has also been used as a cover for the novel, and an iconic photograph of Bela Lugosi still appears on the most recent Oxford World's Classics reprint.[30] This iconography is symptomatic of the incorporation of the novel, *Dracula*, and of the *character* of Count Dracula, not merely into popular consciousness but more particularly into visual culture. By the end of the twentieth century, the distinctions in Anglo-American public consciousness between the contents of Stoker's novel and the individual portrayals of cinematic actors were blurred if not utterly confused. Through cinema, television adaptation, the graphic novel and twentieth-century fictions that appropriated the Count as a character, Dracula became effectively independent of *Dracula*. Only in academic criticism does it seem that the two stand any chance of being successfully reunited.

Translation of *Dracula* into non-Anglophone languages was fairly rapid. Stoker himself wrote a short preface, dated 1898, to the abridged Icelandic edition *Makt Myrkranna* [*Power of Darkness*], published in 1901. The author's characteristic anti-Semitism was evident in this preface, which compared the 'crimes' of the Count to 'the notorious murders of Jacob the disemboweller' – a non-too-subtle assertion of Jewish identity to Jack the Ripper. A German translation, *Dracula: Ein Vampyr-Roman* [*Dracula: A Vampire Novel*] followed in 1908, a Russian-language version, *Graf Drakula: Roman* [*Count Dracula: A Novel*] in c. 1912, and a French translation in 1920. None of these editions, nor indeed the subsequent first translations of the novel into Irish (1933), Italian (1945), Japanese (1956) and Spanish (1962) incorporate any sort of preface or introductory matter.[31] As with the British and American reprints until the 1960s, the novel was simply presented as an entertaining fiction with no deeper cultural or literary significance. *Dracula*, in whatever language, was a work simply marketed for undiscerning readers – the purchasers of pulp paperbacks, moviegoers, US servicemen stationed overseas, bored British teenagers seeking a thrill. It was not a student text, and had no place in academic reading, let alone in scholarly writing.

The rise of the specifically scholarly – as opposed to the unequivocally popular – edition of *Dracula* reflects the novel's gradual integration, from the 1960s, into critical as well as entertainment culture. The eroticism of British and American cinematic adaptations in this period was pivotal. The films of the 1960s in particular made the connections between the vampire's predation and sexual seduction explicit and unavoidable. In this respect, popular cinema interrogated and interpreted the symbolic possibilities of the novel in a way that anticipated the academic criticism of the 1970s.

Though the first modern critical study of *Dracula* was published as early as 1959, the novel itself did not gain a substantial introduction until as late as 1965. *Dracula* first appeared with explanatory notes – tentative and in some places inaccurate, but still suitable for student use – some ten years later.[32] Both of these publications appeared in the United States, and British publishers seem disinclined for some years to regard *Dracula* as a work likely to sell alongside works of serious, canonical literature. Though Penguin listed a paperback *Dracula* in its catalogue as early as 1979, the first annotated British scholarly edition did not appear until 1983. This latter, with its minimal annotations, inaccurate chronology of Stoker's life and works, and at-times apologetic introduction by A. N. Wilson, was significant only for its cautious admission of *Dracula* to the canon of the Oxford University Press World's Classics series.[33] This was probably the most prestigious imprint to issue the novel in its 86-year history.

Twenty-five years after Wilson's *Dracula*, annotated and scholarly editions of the novel probably outnumber mass-market, text-only paperbacks. Clive Leatherdale's hardback *Dracula Unearthed* (1998) is probably the most extensively annotated; Glennis Byron's 1998 Broadview edition is distinguished by appendices that include contemporary sources and reviews; John Paul Riquelme's 2002 edition for Bedford/St Martin's embodies both scholarly essays and historical contexts; the 2007 Artswork edition has an introduction that surveys the critical field between 1958 and the year of its publication. All of these editions, and others like them, offer different facilities to their readers, from up-to-date critical commentary, to late-Victorian reviews, letters and illustrations. The factor which links them all, though, is the underlying assumption that *Dracula* is a text worthy of both undergraduate study and post-graduate publication. From its critical origins as a work deemed unworthy of its author's literary abilities, *Dracula* has now attained a cultural as well as a cult status. Only the most arid and old-fashioned of critics would now fail to acknowledge Stoker's acceptance within contemporary academia.

DRACULA IN MODERN ACADEMIC CRITICISM

In June 1912, the US edition of the *Bookman* noted that 'Since the death of Bram Stoker several writers in the weekly and daily journals have thought to bestow high praise upon his *Dracula* by saying that it will eventually take its place with Mrs Shelley's *Frankenstein*.'[34] Despite the sentiments expressed in this prescient remark, it was to be some 47 years until *Dracula* became the subject of a systematic, theoretically coherent, critical analysis. This pioneering study, Maurice Richardson's 'The Psychoanalysis of Ghost Stories' (1959), effectively set the agenda for *Dracula* criticism for almost the next three decades. Though it liberated Stoker's novel from critical obscurity, Richardson's article unknowingly served also to restrict what might be said regarding the symbolism of *Dracula*. In addition to precipitating sexuality to a pre-eminent place in the symbolic interpretation of the novel, Richardson's adherence to a psychoanalytical model of the unconscious and his speculations regarding Stoker's private life imposed an abiding theoretical orthodoxy upon the critical works that followed his lead.

Controversially, Richardson was unequivocal that *Dracula* must be studied 'From a Freudian standpoint' because 'from no other does the story really make any sense'.[35] Richardson's critical certainty effectively deflects critical attention away from the literal surface of the novel, passing over both the narrative and its depiction of contemporary thought in favour of a sexual symbolism that may have been traumatic and unconscious rather than knowingly deployed by Stoker. As subsequent criticism has indeed demonstrated, *Dracula* may 'make sense' from any one of a number of perspectives, cultural and material as well as psychoanalytical. It must be said, though, that Richardson's lead, in terms of both a sexual focus and a broadly psychoanalytical methodology, was followed by the majority of *Dracula* critics throughout the 1970s and into the 1980s. Richardson, certainly, associates the theory with the detail in such a way as to enforce a credible (though not invariably convincing) case. His work, in rapid succession, associates the narrative with 'Guilt', incest, and the involuntary expression of 'infantile sexuality': 'There is an obvious fixation at the oral level, with all that sucking and biting, also a generous allowance of anality'.[36] The Count, also, is in psychoanalytical terms 'a father-figure of huge potency'.[37] Hence, Richardson's suggestion that, in psychoanalytical terms, all of Stoker's characters are symbolically members of one family, allows the novel to be both 'a quite blatant demonstration of the Oedipus Complex' and a literary re-enactment of the 'Primal Crime' of Freud's *Totem and Taboo*, in which patricide is the outcome of 'the brothers banding together against the father who has tried to keep all the females to himself'.[38] The enduring influence of Richardson is evident in later studies specifically aimed at a student readership: David Punter's analysis of *Dracula* in *The Literature of Terror* (1980) and Phyllis Roth's reading of the breadth of Stoker's works in her *Bram Stoker* (1982), in particular, represent successful and persuasive responses to Richardson's at-times polemical reading.[39]

Psychoanalysis, however, is not monolithic, and Richardson's assertions did not remain unchallenged from within his own theoretical field. Phyllis Roth, in particular, undermined the assumption of an underlying Oedipal motivation for the novel through her suggestion that the strong family alliances identified by Richardson were both fractured and indicative of an ambivalent relationship with the vampire. As she suggests,

> the split between the sexual vampire family and the asexual Van Helsing group is not at all clear-cut: Jonathan, Van Helsing, Seward and Holmwood are all overwhelmingly attracted to the vampires, to sexuality. Fearing this, they employ two defenses, projection and denial: it is not we who want the vampires, it is they who want us (to eat us, to seduce us, to kill us).[40]

Indeed, the graphic violence actually *witnessed* by the reader is enacted only by the mortal opponents of the Count: the killings of the child offered to the vampiric trio, of the child's mother, of the sailors on the *Demeter*, of Mr Swales and the attack that leads to Renfield's death occur away from the reader's gaze. For Roth, the wish to kill, to consume, to possess is projected onto the vampire, while being enacted by his self-righteous opponents. In a sense, as she concludes, the novel is pre-Oedipal rather than Oedipal: through the oral motif it anticipates possession rather than attempting to assert it after traumatic loss.[41]

Many of the assertions of psychoanalytical criticism are as dependent upon the biography of the novel's author as they are upon the so-called unconscious of the text itself. This psychobiography characteristically projects *Dracula* as a uniquely intense and involuntary expression of traumatic though repressed memories from the author's youthful and adult life. Stoker's childhood, his self-confessed infantile debilitation and his large family have all served as a focus for psychobiography. Seymour Shuster, for example, considers the vampire to be a representation of an unnamed medical professional who bled Stoker during his long childhood illness.[42] Joseph Bierman, alternatively, argues that the novel reflects an unspeakable sibling rivalry on the part of its author, the evidence being 'three instances of infanticide by eating and sucking', as well as some strikingly oblique references to his brothers' names in the plot.[43] Finally, in an intriguing twist on the Freudian Primal Father, first suggested by Richardson, Daniel Lapin interprets the Count as a representation of Stoker's own father who (Lapin claims) routinely sexually abused the author and his siblings of both sexes.[44] Though provocative, these assertions depend upon somewhat sparse evidence: a few autobiographical lines in Stoker's biography of Irving, the unsupported opinions of biographers writing for a popular rather than scholarly readership, the assumption that Stoker's mid- to late-Victorian psyche can be satisfactorily mapped onto post-Victorian models of the mind. A degree of caution should, necessarily, be encouraged on the part of the reader.

Stoker's marriage is another focus of psychobiography, in part as a consequence of one biographer's insistence that, according to family tradition, the author's wife was reluctant to engage in sexual intercourse following the birth of their only child.[45] Penelope Shuttle and Peter Redgrove, for example, contend that Florence Stoker suffered a painful menstrual cycle, and queries whether this 'gave Stoker's subliminal mind the hint that formulated a myth of formidable power, out of the ferocity of a frustrated bleeding woman, crackling with energy and unacknowledged sexuality'.[46] The sexuality of Bram Stoker, according to his biographer and great-nephew Daniel Farson, was deflected by his wife's apparent frigidity towards prostitutes: as Farson confides, 'I know that he "enjoyed" the reputation of being a "womaniser", reputedly famous for his sexual exploits.'[47] This claim, though, is never substantiated, and Farson's most controversial assertion, that 'Bram's writing showed signs of guilt and sexual frustration' because 'He probably caught syphilis around the turn of the century, possibly as early as the year of *Dracula*, 1897', is far from universally accepted.[48]

The problem with any psychoanalytical or psychobiographical interpretation is the lack of sure evidence supporting the existence of mental trauma, and, indeed, the theoretical assumption that that the very act of denying a psychosis effectively confirms its unconscious presence. There is no reliable diagnosis of Stoker's childhood illness, nor any record that he enjoyed anything other than cordial relations with his father and siblings. There is no evidence, beyond the lack of a second child, that the Stokers suffered sexual problems or marital difficulties. There was no sexual scandal associated with the author during his lifetime, and his death certificate is ambiguous enough to suggest the presence of Bright's Disease, a kidney disorder, as much as it might syphilis.[49] Changing academic attitudes towards the reliability of psychoanalytical diagnoses, as much as fashions in criticism itself, have thus seen the broadly Freudian consensus on *Dracula* challenged by the rise of cultural materialism in particular.

In place of the twentieth-century models of the mind imposed upon *Dracula*, its characters and author by psychoanalysis, recent criticism has deployed a thoroughly Victorian psychology. This psychology is not exclusively that of Lombroso, meticulously demonstrated by Victor Sage and Ernest Fontana in the 1980s. *Dracula* has also been considered as a work shaped by the physiological model of the mind associated with William Carpenter and signified in the novel by sporadic reference to the processes of 'unconscious cerebration' – the unconscious but reliable working of a mind otherwise occupied by conscious thought. The work of David Glover and William Hughes in particular popularized this approach to the novel in the last decade of the twentieth century, though David Hume Flood's underread 1989 article on the physiology of the blood transfusions within *Dracula* is equally worthy of consideration.[50] Other issues that have preoccupied critics have included the practices – clinical and occult – of hypnotism, the pseudosciences of phrenology and physiognomy, and the novel's implication in the contemporary treatment of, and attitudes towards, dead and diseased bodies.[51] The precedent set by readings of the medical script of *Dracula* have been echoed by readings of other professional discourses discernible within both *Dracula* and the author's biography: the law, a profession which Stoker studied but never practised, has proved one such focus.[52]

If the methodologies associated with cultural materialism have challenged the theoretical primacy of psychoanalysis in the criticism of *Dracula*, so, too, have alternative interpretations undermined the centrality of the novel's perceived sexual symbolism. The initial suggestion that *Dracula* was a vehicle whereby sexual fears may be both satisfactorily expressed and safely discharged has come under scrutiny. The novel continues to retain its capacity to express dis-ease in criticism, though the focus has increasingly shifted away from sexuality and towards questions of racial and national identity.

The novel's capacity for exploring fears of invasion and national decline have been acknowledged for some time. However, the clear-cut oppositions between east and west that structure so many of these analyses have been questioned by the relatively recent (and by no means unanimous) integration of Stoker into the Irish studies canon. Stoker's acceptance as an Irish writer (as opposed to a British writer, or even a Gothic writer) has been historically inhibited by his long residence in London, and his fictional engagement with British rather than Irish locales and characters.[53] Nonetheless, *Dracula* became a novel increasingly cited in writings both about Irish-authored fiction, and in those concerned with the fictionalization of Victorian Irish culture and politics, from the mid-1990s. In such critical works, the conventional polarities of invader and invaded, east and west, are often strikingly reversed. Ireland is the west, England the east, and so the invader may well be symbolically, as Terry Eagleton argues, the absentee landlord, an alien colonist eager to suck the vitality out of a fruitful land.[54] In this mythology, as Seamus Deane suggests, the vanquishing of the vampire represents the rise of a nationalist alternative and the driving of the oppressor back to its own country. There he will face death, and then take on a legendary status which perpetuates not his own fame but that of the brave and far-sighted few who have resisted his invasion.[55]

Mythological interpretations of *Dracula* such as those by Eagleton and Deane are arguably as much part of modern political polemic as they are associated with literary criticism. Their claim to accuracy, though, is rendered questionable by Stoker's biography. Though it is tempting to see a form of nascent nationalism in Stoker's confession that he was, in the nineteenth century, 'a philosophical Home Ruler', nothing could arguably be further from the truth. As David Glover suggests, Stoker's politics were Liberal rather than nationalist, and his vision of Ireland connected to a benevolent British paternalism rather than nationalistic self-determination.[56] There is certainly an Irish input to *Dracula*, and indeed an *Irish Gothic* heritage, as Glover notes.[57] *Dracula*, however, does not translate easily and unequivocally into a novel of nationalistic aspirations – at least in a specifically Irish context: as more than one critic has suggested, the Count may as easily function as a metaphor for the Balkan question as for the Irish one.[58]

It is worth noting that the Irish studies critique of *Dracula* has entered into a relative decline in recent years. The interpretation of political and nationalistic symbolism within the novel at the turn of the twenty-first century has become centred upon the east of Europe rather than the Irish west: one might note here the readings of the eastern European implications of Stoker's work made by Vesna Goldsworthy, Eleni Coundouriotis and Matthew Gibson, as well as the political implications of the novel's later translation, discussed by S. T. Gürçaglar.[59] Future criticism will no doubt further disperse and relocate the potential political symbolism of Stoker's novel.

Perhaps the most enduring focus for *Dracula* criticism, though, is gender. Its presence is implicit in the earliest Freudian studies of bodies desired, despised and possessed. It is more explicitly addressed in those analyses concerned with the deployment of sexual symbolism. It informs the rhetoric of a body politic shot through with institutional sexism, and is integrated into the definitions of approved behaviour and deviance imposed within the novel from both medical and social standpoints. Finally, gender has been comprehensively written into the biography and psychobiography of Stoker as a preoccupation whose influence may be discerned in both his writings and his public life.

Criticism has considered the depiction of the New Woman through Mina not merely as a straightforward polemic against feminism but also as an index of the author's ambivalent response to assertive or independent women. Biographical details cited in support of the latter assertion include Stoker's marriage to a socially ambitious wife and his relationship with a mother who – if family legend is to be believed – once chopped off the hand of a burglar.[60] Independent women punctuate Stoker's fiction, from Norah Joyce in *The Snake's Pass*, who saves the hero from death, to Betty Pole in *Miss Betty*, who deliberately confronts a highwayman, to Teuta in *The Lady of the Shroud*, who takes up arms to defend her father and her Balkan nation. Heroines whose assertiveness is more obviously sexual may be found in *The Mystery of the Sea* and *Lady Athlyne*. The common factor that links all of these female figures, and which connects them also to Mina Harker, is their eventual surrender to male protection, their abdication of independence of action, if not of thought also.[61] Though Daniel Farson suggests that Stoker, allegedly repelled by his ambitious and forceful wife, developed an 'infatuation with the ideal woman, so unnaturally feminine, so vulnerable to attack', one might see here a darker fantasy in which the powerful woman is tamed, rendered secondary to, and dependent upon, a male whose power and public status enhanced by her surrender.[62]

The relationship between the male vampire and his female victims is perhaps, however, the most important recurrent focus of the gendered critique of *Dracula*. Despite the substantial number of interpretations of this relationship, an abiding consensus exists among critics regarding the innate and latent sexuality enjoyed by the two heroines. Alan Johnson's argument is representative. As he notes,

> each woman develops . . . a life of conscious and willing conformity to her society and yet also a life of largely subconscious rebellion against it. In the case of each woman, Dracula symbolises her inner rebelliousness, and its crisis coincides with her commerce with Dracula.[63]

The Count, notably, symbolizes but does not initiate their 'subconscious rebellion' against individual and sexual conformity: he is 'a symbolic double of each woman's rebellious egoism' rather than its origin.[64] Effectively he liberates things that are already there: as Phyllis Roth suggests, 'Only when Lucy becomes a vampire is she allowed to be "voluptuous", yet she must have been so long before, judging from her effect on men and from Mina's descriptions of her.'[65] Though consensus locates Mina as much as Lucy within this assumption of a latent sexuality somehow authorized by the vampire's intervention, her position is arguably more equivocal: certainly, her consciousness is more inclined to be shocked by Lucy's potentially indecorous nocturnal behaviour at Whitby on a night which the two 'never refer to' (138).[66]

If women are innately sexual beings, and sexuality is associated with the 'deviant' vampire, then a form of aggression against women – such as that undertaken by Holmwood in the London churchyard, or by Van Helsing in Dracula's castle, appears to be justified within the confines of the novel. The novel here evades the chivalry of Stoker's gentlemanliness, disqualifying the sexual woman *as a woman*, and authorizing interventions that literally pin her back into passivity. Passivity, as Christopher Craft notes, is a façade, and when it is breached the certain identities, the distinctive demarcations, of the two complementary genders are confused and even conflated.[67] In a sense, the vampire hunters are forced to come together in a form of homosocial union because the females who they love and defend become at times unrecognizable. Implicitly, they recognize the enduring stability and fixity of their own gendered identity – an identity which the 'effeminate' Harker progressively 'grows into' – as something far more reliable than the mobile and dualistic entity that is the vampirized (and sexually liberated) female. Indeed, it is plausible to suggest that the men in *Dracula* are closer to each other than they could ever to be to any woman within the novel, once they have witnessed the transformations of both Lucy and Mina.

The homosocial collusion of males against both the vampire and his female acolytes is not necessarily a homosexual one – though more than one reading has discussed the possibility of Stoker's novel containing a homosexual script.[68] As earlier psychoanalytical criticism has asserted, though, the vampire may exert an attractiveness for the men despite their revulsion at his actions – and may further be the source of gender confusion. Christopher Craft, notably, explores this through the confused signification of the vampire's mouth – an opening which is replicated elsewhere in the novel through the equally hungry mouths of the female vampires. Craft asserts:

As the primary site of erotic experience in *Dracula*, this mouth equivocates, giving the lie to the easy separation of the masculine and the feminine. Luring at first with an inviting orifice, a promise of red softness, but delivering instead a piercing bone, the vampire mouth fuses and confuses . . . the gender-based categories of the penetrating and the receptive . . . .

Indeed, this conflation poses what Craft considers to be a number of 'disturbing questions': 'Are we male or are we female? Do we have penetrators or orifices? And if both, what does that mean?'[69] The fearful thing is that the group know the answer to these questions, even where they would rather not confront them. Craft rightly states of *Dracula* that 'the sexual threat that this novel first evokes, manipulates, sustains but never finally represents is that Dracula will seduce, penetrate, drain another male'.[70] If he can do this, and his victims will be compelled to do it in turn, then it is inevitable that a further male–male encounter will sooner or later take place: with the death of Lucy, Holmwood, Seward and Morris have no convenient female partner to form the first object of their vampiric desires, once initiated. Even Van Helsing effectively has no wife, she being in Amsterdam and 'dead to me, though alive by church's law, though no wits, all gone' (219). They are thus men fearful of a different dimension of closeness, of a crossing of a bloody, penetrative boundary which they, as much as the reader, know may symbolize a sexual encounter. When enacted between men and women, such symbolic exchanges of blood may be 'a sweet and comforting idea' (219), a substitute for the rarefied and sanctioned sexuality permitted within marriage. Between men alone, though, they symbolize quite another type of penetration. This fear is so strong that it arguably determines the final moments of the Count. His death is neither as orgasmically graphic as that of Lucy, nor as emphatically phallic. Arguably, even in disposing of the enemy that has confused their clear vision of gender difference, the men fear to be seen penetrating another male. As Christopher Craft suggests, therefore, it is Lucy who 'receives the phallic correction that Dracula deserves'.[71]

Dracula criticism has evolved remarkably over the past 50 years, moving from the margins of the critical establishment to the centre, and from a narrow interpretation through psychoanalysis to a presence in almost all theoretical critiques. It is a novel as amenable to criticism through materialism as it is through psychoanalysis, is as likely to be critically productive in Queer studies as it is under post-colonial scrutiny, and it remains a standard text in the generic criticism associated with Gothic. The most recent bibliography of Stoker criticism, published in 2004, lists in excess of 400 books and articles which consider the author, the vast majority of these being concerned with *Dracula*.[72] This figure has been comfortably exceeded in the past five years, and there is no indication that *Dracula* will not continue to inspire a wide range of responses for the foreseeable future. As has already been suggested, though, the continued vibrancy of *Dracula* scholarship remains as dependent upon the continued scholarly interrogation of the detail of the novel and the further exposure of its contexts, as much as it does upon new theoretical or methodological developments.

CHAPTER 5

ADAPTATION, INTERPRETATION AND INFLUENCE

DRACULA, OR THE UN-DEAD, IN A PROLOGUE AND FIVE ACTS (1897)

Dracula was performed only once as a stage play during Stoker's lifetime. Despite the author's position as a theatrical personality, and the production receiving its première at Irving's Lyceum Theatre on London's Strand, no commentary upon the performance appeared in the press. This was hardly surprising, however. *Dracula, or The Un-Dead*, in a Prologue and Five Acts, was performed on 18 May 1897 – *before* the official release of the novel – quite simply to establish the author's copyright as dramatist as well as novelist. The first staged production of *Dracula* may therefore have been little more than a stilted reading through of dialogue, and a rudimentary enacting of scenes, both being lifted more or less directly from the novel. As only two people actually paid the unusually high fee of one guinea to attend the performance, the printed programme issued for *Dracula* by the Lyceum would appear to be justified only in its status as evidence of the performance having taken place.[1]

Stoker was a keen advocate of the property rights of authors, taking pains to establish copyright of his novels in Britain and the United States, and working with the London-based Society of Authors on behalf of other writers. His widow became a member of the Society in 1922, in order to utilize the organization's legal knowledge in defence of her inherited rights over *Dracula*.[2] Stoker's decision to formally establish his rights over *Dracula* as a play was a sound and far-sighted one, though it is doubtful whether he could have anticipated, in 1897, that theatrical copyright would ultimately apply also to the then nascent and largely unproven medium of cinema. Whatever the case, Stoker appears to have taken no interest in the drama of *Dracula* after its only production. It was to be Florence Stoker, the author's widow, who was to reap the rewards of Stoker's prescience – a modest though significant financial gain based first upon two stage productions and latterly on a black-and-white talking picture distributed across the world. Her assertion of copyright, though, was further to shape the cinematic vampire in a way that was arguably as influential as the innovations proposed by directors and film studios in the United States and beyond. In a sense, part of the authorship of the derivative, replicated twentieth-century *Dracula* must be attributed to Florence, rather than Bram, Stoker.

NOSFERATU, EINE SYMPHONIE DES GRAUENS (1922)

Though Stoker may have been involved in discussions regarding an authorized stage production of his novel as early as 1899, the first appearance of *Dracula* as a commercial production was an unauthorized and deliberately mistitled film shot by the German director F. W. Murnau. *Nosferatu, Eine Symphonie des Grauens* [*Nosferatu, a Symphony of Horrors*], a silent film claimed by its producers to be 'freely adapted' from Stoker's novel, was filmed on location in 1921, and shown first in Berlin on 4 March 1922.[3] The film has been hailed as a masterpiece of German Expressionism, though Murnau's production departs from the artificial, geometric interiors that characterize other films in the Expressionist genre. *Nosferatu* does, however, retain the Expressionist commitment to the 'visual, metaphorical and mythic' rather than the naturalistic or mimetic, and as such might be said to reflect the troubled consciousness of post-Armistice Germany as much as it does the dis-ease of Stoker's late-Victorian Britain.[4]

   The plot of *Nosferatu* was considerably more simple than either Stoker's novel or, indeed, the five-act drama which was probably unknown to Murnau and his associates at Prana-Film. As David Skal's assessment suggests, the film's screenwriter, Henrik Galeen, presented Murnau with a shooting script that might well have escaped Florence Stoker's notice had the programme for *Nosferatu* not explicitly asserted its consanguinity with *Dracula*. Galeen

   changed all the characters' names – Count Dracula became Graf Orlock; Harker was now Hutter, Mina was called Ellen, Van Helsing renamed Bulwer, etc., – and simplified the plot while retaining the basic structure – the young man's journey to Transylvania to sell a house to a vampire, the creature's sea-voyage to the young man's town and subsequent possession of his wife, and the intervention of a patriarchal scientist to reveal the nature of the vampire pestilence.[5]

The specificity of time and space that characterize Stoker's record-intensive novel were also disrupted in *Nosferatu* by the imposition of a vaguely European backdrop, and an atemporality which facilitates the juxtaposition of an apparently Eastern peasant culture with more Western mercantile seaboard architecture. Whitby and London are condensed into an old-fashioned European port – variously Bremen or Wisport – whose quays are bordered by gabled, Dutch-style townhouses. At the behest of his employer (who is no longer Hawkins but Knock – a version of Renfield), Hutter travels from this port through a picturesque European 'Mittel Land' (47), stopping at an old inn frequented by gypsies. Travelling onward, he is taken up by Orlock's coach, a shrouded, spasmodically moving vehicle whose strangeness is innovatively enhanced in the film though being shot in negative.

At Graf Orlock's castle Hutter is greeted, and subsequently assaulted, by the 'nosferatu' (281) or vampire himself – played, with simultaneous camp and menace by the German actor Max Schreck.[6] Schreck's portrayal follows the precedent of Stoker's novel to a certain extent – the actor's prosthetic make-up gives the character a Semitic nose, and his prominent bushy eyebrows are made all the more emphatic by the facial pallor associated with 1920s monochrome film stock. It is the phallic nature of the vampire's figure, that is most suggestive, however. Schreck's vampire lacks both the profuse grey hair of Stoker's Count, and apparently fails to grow younger as he absorbs the substance of his victims. Orlock's long, shaven head is surrounded by the seemingly angular planes of his cheek-bones and jaw line, these possibly being as prosthetic as his nose, pointed ears and extended fingernails. His dark frock coat is seemingly cut to emphasize his height and thinness, as well as to exaggerate the pallor of his face and hands, and the dark circles surrounding his eyes. Orlock's fangs are placed centrally in his mouth, and this detail connects him emphatically to the plague-carrying rodents who accompany him to Hutter's home town rather than simply to Stoker's canine-fanged vampire (63). The vampire in *Nosferatu* would seem to be an associate of insidious disease rather than of red-toothed predation. The phallic nature of Orlock is further suggested by his behaviour on board the ship which carries him to Hutter's home town: he is seen to rise, like an immense penis, from his coffin, and his evident interest in the sailors (and earlier interest in Hutter) is only partially offset by his desire for Hutter's wife, Ellen, whose existence he first discovers through a miniature in the possession of her husband.

Following the scenes in the castle, Murnau condenses the plot of *Dracula*, passing rapidly over Hutter's illness and escape, and the voyage of the vampire, in order to bring Orlock to Ellen's bedside. Though the novel does feature a Van Helsing figure in Bulwer – a figure who appears to have an unhealthy interest in abnormal biology – it is Hutter's wife, informed by a treatise on vampires, that finally despatches the vampire. The sexual implications of vampirism are again accorded due prominence in Murnau's adaptation. As David Skal notes, Ellen learns from her vampire book that 'the vampire can be defeated only if a virtuous woman willingly lets him remain with her until dawn'.[7] This sets Ellen at odds with Mina, who *attempts* to declare herself a far less willing victim in *Dracula* and who, in any case, is attacked while semi-conscious and not able to make a reasoned judgement. Murnau in effect develops the potential of Stoker's Mina in his later Ellen. She becomes not simply a victim, but a martyr also – and her selfless self-assertion is the central action through which the vampire is defeated. No man excludes her from the campaign against vampiric invasion.

The vampire, in *Nosferatu*, loses even more of the limited freedom which Van Helsing accords him in *Dracula* (283–4): though Orlock throws shadows (cf. 283) that seem to roam in a manner strangely independent of his bodily movements, he cannot walk in daylight like Stoker's Count (215). The virtuous woman who seduces him therefore provokes his death as the cock crows and daylight enters the marital bedchamber. In Murnau's film, the dying vampire simply fades into the light; in later film adaptations his demise will be characteristically spectacular and gory. Murnau's suggestion, not found in Stoker's *Dracula*, that light is fatal to vampires was, however, to become a standard that influenced both cinematic and novelistic depictions of the vampire from the 1930s to the present.

Florence Stoker, who knew of *Nosferatu* but had not apparently seen the film, was still far from impressed by its artistic innovation and technical ingenuity. As an unauthorized production it would not bring her any royalties, and its presence would no doubt deter any entrepreneur producer desirous of making an authorized *Dracula*. Though Prana-Film had gone into receivership by June 1922, Florence Stoker pressed the Society of Authors to take action on her behalf. If she could not gain financial compensation, she could at least have *Nosferatu* removed from distribution, thus freeing the way for an authorized, and royalty paying, successor. Though she eventually won her case, and had the original print of *Nosferatu* destroyed, copies in various states of completion continued to circulate in Europe and the United States as late as 1929. In effect, though Florence Stoker had regained control of the *name* of *Dracula* by 1925, the alluring body of the vampire, and the motif of a vampire count, continued to circulate independently of both Stoker's novel and her own desire for control of what was, by 1924, a nascent theatrical franchise.[8]

DRACULA, BY HAMILTON DEANE (1924)

It was during the prosecution of *Nosferatu* that Florence Stoker became involved in negotiations that would lead to an authorized stage production. Hamilton Deane, an Irish actor who had toured with Henry Irving's Vacation Company in 1899, approached the author's widow with his own adaptation of the novel for the London and provincial stages.[9] The proposed script was heavily cut in comparison to Stoker's own 1897 production, and the tone was melodramatic rather than truly Gothic. As Harry Ludlam, an associate of Deane's, recalls:

> He cut out entirely the first portion of the book, including Jonathan Harker's nerve-wracking experiences in Dracula's castle in Transylvania, and brought the vampire horror right to the heart of London from the opening curtain, by setting the first act in Harker's house in Hampstead. He wrote the drama in three acts, two being played in Harker's study and the third in Mina Harker's boudoir. Then a sensational epilogue, in which Count Dracula was tracked to his coffin at Carfax and gruesomely transfixed by Van Helsing's purging stake.[10]

The play's epilogue may not, however, have been as graphic as Ludlam suggests. The Lord Chamberlain apparently granted a licence for the performance of Deane's stage play with the sole proviso that the Count's death should be enacted out of sight of the audience.[11]

Another major innovation was the styling of the Count as a gentleman in outline rather than as an instantly recognizable degenerate. Deane's vampire wore contemporary evening dress – the white tie, tail coat and opera cloak that remains a signifier of vampirism to the present – rather than the frogged frock coat of Graf Orlock, or the unexceptional dress effected by Stoker's Count. Seward's perception of the Count as 'a tall, thin man, clad in black' (325), and Harker's depiction of his host as being 'clad in black from head to foot, without a single speck of colour about him anywhere' (56) both serve to emphasize the central signification of the Count's pallid, strikingly featured face. Deane's vampire, however, presents a more rounded threat. The vampire is now not merely a figure so unexceptional that it could move without comment across London, but is also aligned with the establishment, with domestic signifiers of power and wealth rather than with visible foreignness.

Deane's adaptation received its first performance at the Grand Theatre in Derby in June 1924. It was a notable success, and the Company toured with the production across the British provinces, prior to its West End premier at the Little Theatre on the Strand on 14 February 1927. Despite the popularity of *Dracula* with provincial audiences and the provincial press, the London critics were hostile. The capital's audiences, though, were more receptive, and the play ran for 200 performances at the Little Theatre and a further 391 at the Prince of Wales' Theatre.[12] The financial success – though not necessarily the style of adaptation – of Deane's production attracted the attention of the US impresario and publisher Horace Liveright, during a visit to London in 1927. Though Florence Stoker had commissioned a further – and unsuccessful – adaptation of *Dracula* from the dramatist Charles Morrell in 1927, she was apparently receptive to the overtures made by Liveright, and a further revision was commissioned from the American dramatist John L. Balderston. Balderston's production received its official launch at New York's Fulton Theatre on 5 October 1927, with the Hungarian actor Bela Lugosi in the title role.[13] This casting signalled a further significant change to the already modified Count of Deane's production: as David Skal suggests,

> The London Dracula was middle-aged and malignant; Lugosi presented quite a different picture: sexy, continental, with slicked-back patent-leather hair and a weird green cast to his makeup – a Latin lover from beyond the grave, Valentino gone slightly rancid.

It was a combination that worked, and audiences – especially female audiences – relished, even wallowed in, the romantic paradoxes.[14]

Dracula was again a narrative of sexual rather than merely dramatic interest. The Count had become as perceptibly provocative to the audience as he had once been to Stoker's Mina (331). The logic of the mass market dictated that this would be the formula to shape the next cinematic adaptation of *Dracula*.

THE UNIVERSAL *DRACULA* (1931)

Though not the studio's first choice, Lugosi was to play the vampire in the first authorized film of *Dracula*, released by Universal on 12 February 1931.[15] At times heated negotiations between Liveright, Florence Stoker and the studio, apparently brokered by the gentlemanly Lugosi, had resulted in a contract, signed in 1930, which conveyed the rights to Universal for $40,000 and placed the director Tod Browning in charge of the production. Florence Stoker's royalties, though significant, were but a fraction of what the film, and its Universal successors under the *Dracula* franchise, were to produce even before her control over the copyright had expired.[16]

The 1931 film was to restore to mass public consciousness some elements of *Dracula* which had necessarily been removed from the British and American stage productions. Renfield, rather than Harker, travels by carriage to Transylvania, and there meets the three female vampires, two dark, one (comparatively) fair. Renfield's experiences at the castle account for his later madness in London, and his peculiar relationship to the Count. Indeed, he returns to England on the Count's ship. Other characters were renamed or remodelled. Mina Harker becomes Mina Seward; Lucy Westenra becomes the more easily pronounced Lucy Western (strangely, without the symbolic associations of the name discerned in Stoker's novel by subsequent critics).[17] The Count becomes a welcome guest of the Seward household, and Van Helsing suspects the visitor's vampiric nature on discovering that he casts no reflection on the surface of a polished cigarette case. He does, however, cast a shadow. His demise occurs off-screen, signified by a succession of theatrical groans.

The enduring influence of the 1931 Universal *Dracula*, like that of *Nosferatu*, cannot be underestimated. Indeed, Universal purchased a copy of Murnau's film, despite the potential illegality involved, in order to consider it as a basis for their own adaptation of the Balderston play, rewritten for the studio by the Pulitzer-Prize winning novelist, Louis Bromfield. Even though the 1931 *Dracula* was a talking picture, Lugosi's eastern-inflected English, learned phonetically and sparsely but emphatically spoken, inspired a generation of Counts to be scarce-spoken rather than effusive. This recalls Stoker's novel. Though the Count discourses extensively to Harker, he says comparatively little when he is in London, and in any case is overwhelmingly a figure reported by others, rather than one who enjoys frequent access to the surface of the narrative in his own right. Lugosi's catch-phrases, too, have become clichés to be repeated and recognized in cinematic and novelistic revisions of the vampire, irrespective of whether they draw upon Stoker's novel or Bromfield's script. His characteristic greeting, the heavily accented 'Good evening', for example, is regarded as an 'instinctive' part of vampire culture in Jeffrey N. McMahan's *Vampires Anonymous* (1991), just as his admission that he 'doesn't drink – *wine!*' is mockingly parodied by the vampires in Poppy Z. Brite's 1992 novel, *Lost Souls*.[18] Lugosi's image, indeed, remained iconic even after his death and the production of later films with other actors cast in the role of Dracula. The Hungarian actor, indeed, became a victim of this association, finding that theatrical and cinematic employers would offer him little other than vampire roles – roles that towards the end of his career descended into comedy and parody. Lugosi died in 1956, and was buried in his coffin in his opera cloak, evening dress and the medallion which he had worn to greet Harker on the steps of Castle Dracula.[19]

Universal's possession of the rights for *Dracula* ensured that recognizable adaptations of (or fictional projections from) Stoker's novel were confined to that studio's output. Universal was to produce a number of derivative sequels: *Dracula's Daughter* in 1936, written by Balderston; *Son of Dracula*, starring Lon Chaney junior in 1943; *House of Dracula*, with John Carradine as Count Dracula (or Baron Latos). The Count, again played by John Carradine, was also to appear in Universal's 1944 film, *House of Frankenstein* – an early example of how novelistic boundaries may become blurred in cinematic adaptation. Other studios were to capitalize upon the success of the Universal *Dracula*, and, indeed, upon the iconography popularized by Lugosi, though without legal recourse to the evocative name. Lugosi, for example, was to play Count Mora in garb almost identical to that which he wore as Count Dracula in *Mark of the*

Vampire (1935) directed by Tod Browning for MGM, and with Guy Endore, author of *The Werewolf of Paris* (1933), as one of the screenwriters.

Universal's loss of control over the *Dracula* franchise, though, is signalled not so much by the two comedy films made by Bela Lugosi – *Abbott and Costello Meet Frankenstein* and *Old Mother Riley Meets the Vampire* – in 1948 and 1952 respectively, but rather through the first non-Western cinematic adaptation of Stoker's novels, the 1953 Turkish film *Drakula Istanbulda*. The name and the image of the vampire were now not merely public property but international currency: they had begun to assimilate to the political and social conditions of other cultures, and had expanded the signification of the vampire, his mission and his defeat, in consequence. In this early transfer to the Muslim east of a European figure, enmeshed in the politics of the west and the religious practices of Christianity, can be seen the germs of later revisions of the *Dracula* narrative beyond white Western identities. One should note in this context not merely the 'blaxploitation' films *Blacula* (1972) and *Scream, Blacula, Scream* (1973), which explore issues of slavery and, the second case, of reincarnation and voodoo, but also titles such as *The Seven Brothers Meet Dracula* (1974), a UK-backed production for the Hong Kong market.[20]

By 1956 *Dracula* had become a television drama in the United States, with John Carradine in the title role, and a year later United Artists were to produce the first openly acknowledged adaptation of the novel beyond Universal's control. This latter, significantly, was titled *The Return of Dracula* (and was later retitled *The Curse of Dracula*). Seemingly, the title *Dracula* in isolation did not signify enough novelty to US audiences, some preface or suffix being deemed necessary to distinguish the newer work from that which came before.

THE HAMMER *DRACULA* (1958)

The name of *Dracula*, in bold isolation upon posters and tickets, did however retain the cachet of originality in the United Kingdom, where Deane had continued to perform his own and Balderston's stage adaptations to packed theatrical houses until 1941.[21] The first British cinema adaptation was to come in 1958, the year of Deane's death. The Hammer Films *Dracula*, directed by Terence Fisher, was notably retitled *Horror of Dracula* for its US release. The casting of the Hammer film, though, was to make lasting reputations for its leading actors in much the same way as Universal's 1931 *Dracula* had done for Lugosi. Christopher Lee, a London-born and public-school-educated actor, was chosen to play a saturnine, menacing and darkly sexual Count Dracula, with Peter Cushing as a driven and not always avuncular Van Helsing.

Jimmy Sangster's script for the Hammer *Dracula* was a cause of tension for Lee in particular. In a 1993 interview the actor suggested that:

> within the limitations of the script on the first one *Dracula* (1958) [*sic*] – they disintegrated over the years – I tried to present Stoker's character as he described him in the book. Now that was not done correctly physically, or visually either. And I might have brought the book down on occasions desperately trying to get some of Stoker's lines out in the scene which, over the years, I think I managed to do about three or four times. They were pretty short ones, too. Because this was to me, as an actor playing the part, the great disappointment – that for some extraordinary reason, having written a good script, they chose to ignore Stoker's lines and dialogue almost totally.[22]

Critical opinion is divided as to whether this is 'a good script', however. It is, admittedly, spectacular, and enhanced the reputation as a popular studio committed to the production of what were then described as 'X Certificate' films – which, surprisingly, recalling the modern equivalent of the '18' Certificate, were in the 1950s apparently considered suitable for those aged *16* and above. Its relationship to Stoker's novel, though, as Lee's recollections suggest, is often implicit rather than integral. It is an adaptation and a development of Stoker's plot rather than its reproduction.

Fisher's production drew upon the audience's prior experience of both vampire films and their implicit knowledge of the plot of *Dracula* – a knowledge, no doubt, based in many cases upon cinematic adaptation rather than any first-hand contact with Stoker's novel. Liberties were certainly taken with Stoker's plot. Harker, for example, was no longer a solicitor but an associate of Van Helsing. Van Helsing, in turn, is engaged in a campaign against the Count before the novel opens. Harker is bitten in Transylvania, and in England the roles of Mina and Lucy are exchanged, a sibling relationship between

Holmwood and Lucy (who is also Harker's fiancée) disarming the class tensions apparent in Stoker's novel. Seward and Renfield do not appear at all in the Hammer *Dracula*.

As in *Nosferatu*, the Count is eventually destroyed by sunlight, Van Helsing driving the vampire into the full glare of the sun by dextrous use of the sign of the Cross. The elemental ashes left behind by the vampire, though, were to be regenerated in future Hammer sequels, thus adding further to the myth of reincarnation and rejuvenation left incomplete by the unsatisfactory ritual disposal of the Count in Stoker's novel. More importantly, though, even within the limitations of the 1950s X Certificate, the Hammer *Dracula* made truly graphic that which was merely suggestive in Stoker's novel. In the words of Matthew Bunson, the Hammer *Dracula* is 'colorful, gory, sexy and well-paced', and Lee's performance in particular 'made fangs, red eyes, great amounts of blood, and an overt sexual component an essential part of subsequent vampire films'.[23]

Hammer, like Universal, subsequently exploited their initial production through a range of sequels whose plots departed further and further from both Stoker's novel and its Victorian setting. Lee, in particular, was emphatic:

> As far as my character was concerned, there was some Stoker in the first one, and not in the second (*Dracula – Prince of Darkness*, 1965), because I refused to speak the lines of the script which is why there is no dialogue . . . And then progressively over the next three or four, whatever there were I did for them [*sic*], there was less and less meaning to it. And I kept on saying, well look, here's the book, look at these great lines, look at these great things. Can't we slip them in somewhere? No. They never agreed and that is why they [the films] became progressively less and less interesting and that is why I was determined to stop them.[24]

Despite the obvious artistic differences between the actor and Hammer – the pointed 'them' and 'they' of the quotation – Lee, apparently reluctantly, appeared in a number of subsequent *Dracula* derivatives, beginning with *Dracula – Prince of Darkness* (1965), and continuing through *Dracula has Risen from the Grave* (1969), *Taste the Blood of Dracula* (1970), *Scars of Dracula* (1970), *Dracula AD 1972* (1972) and *The Satanic Rites of Dracula* (1973). The 'death' of the vampire in each prefigured a resurrection of sorts in the subsequent film, with the Count being submerged in ice water or perforated with the spoke of a broken cartwheel, and even, in *Dracula has Risen from the Grave*, being capable of removing a conventional stake from his own heart. The detailed Victorian backdrops of the earlier Hammer films gave way, in the final two, to modern settings, *The Satanic Rites of Dracula* being as much concerned with the anonymity of corporate business as it is with occult ritual. With the latter film's depiction of the Count not as a feudal eastern invader but rather as a businessman plotting world domination from a darkened office block the British myth of *Dracula*, as it were, has turned full circle. A novel apparently concerned with the cultural dis-ease of the late nineteenth century has evolved into a film that both reflects and prophetically anticipates the concerns of the last 30 years of the twentieth century. In taking on the 'big business' that the Count embodies in *The Satanic Rites of Dracula*, Cushing becomes not so much a representation of the Victorian middle class as an acknowledgement of the 'little man', the individual caught up in the machinations of faceless power and impending, seemingly irresistible, change.

F. F. COPPOLA'S *BRAM STOKER'S DRACULA* (1992)

Dracula was sporadically adapted across the 1980s in a variety of television serials and cinematic derivations, few of which attracted any significant critical attention.[25] The approach of the centenary of the first publication of Stoker's novel in 1997, however, inspired the production of what was to be arguably the most controversial cinematic production since Murnau's *Nosferatu*. Coppola's bold title, however, masks a rather loose adaptation of Stoker's 1897 novel. The novel, indeed, is but one discernible source for the film's revision of *Dracula*. *Bram Stoker's Dracula* is possibly the most systematic and self-conscious of all the cinematic adaptations of Stoker's novel, though its alignment with interpretation in many respects distances it from the less dense texture of the earliest films in particular. It is a film concerned with the process of reading and interpreting Stoker's novel as much as it is with the reproduction of the plot of *Dracula*. Thus, the 1897 *Dracula* takes its place as a source for *Bram Stoker's Dracula* alongside the myth of the 'historical' Dracula, Vlad Tepes (sometimes styled as Vlad the Impaler); next to the visual and plot traditions associated with earlier vampire films; and in conjunction with Stoker's biography and the academic criticism of the novel.

Christopher Lee, who introduced Coppola to the audience attending the French première of *Bram Stoker's Dracula*, recalled that:

> I actually read the script long before they made the film and it was, in terms of the sexual element, pretty strong, to put it mildly. I think a lot was cut. The film looked marvellous. It was a great achievement to make it all in the studio, on stage. But it's not Bram Stoker's story. Part of it is. It's the first time he's [i.e., the Count] been properly killed. But even then, he wasn't killed, if you see what I mean. And it wasn't Stoker's story, and it wasn't Stoker's characters as he described them.[26]

Despite the cuts which Lee suggests were made prior to release, the sexual content of Coppola's film is provocative even in a cinematic culture aware of Hammer's frequent display of the semi-nude female body. In the film's opening sequence, the Count – played throughout by Gary Oldman – is represented as a virile, armour-clad medieval warlord; he presents himself to Harker (who is played by Keanu Reeves), though, in the nineteenth century as a somewhat camp elderly man, clad in oriental silks and sporting a bouffant wig of monstrous proportions. The lingering intimacy with which he shaves Harker, after the solicitor has cut himself with a cutthroat razor, is redolent of homo-erotic seduction.

There is, though, a marked heterosexual eroticism, also, from the start of the solicitor's sojourn at the castle. In the scene in which Harker is menaced by the vampiric trio, the solicitor seems more wakeful than Stoker's ingenuous innocent. The vampires emerge through the divan upon which he is laying, their gauzy harem clothing scarcely concealing their naked breasts. Their sexuality is more explicitly oral, also, than Stoker's euphemistic 'kisses' (79): indeed, one of the trio rips open the buttoned fly of the solicitor's trousers, her head making contact with his groin. The trio consume Harker's blood before they are interrupted by the Count, who addresses them in Romanian. As Van Helsing (played by Anthony Hopkins) later demonstrates, the film varies from the novel in that active, post-mortem vampirism is only imposed when the victim drinks the blood of the vampire – a convention that *Bram Stoker's Dracula* shares with the influential 1976 novel *Interview with the Vampire* by Anne Rice.[27]

Coppola's Lucy (played by Sadie Frost) is more openly sexual than Stoker's novelistic heroine. She trades sexual confidences with Mina

(Winona Ryder), in a considerably more explicit manner than is suggested by the 'secrets' (97) they share in the novel, and teasingly toys
with Morris's Bowie knife in a way that emphasizes its already obvious phallic symbolism.[28] When the Count, in a guise more bestial
than elegant, predates upon her in her London garden he appears
to engage in cunnilingus rather than a more decorous neck-biting.
Coppola's Mina, too, is more sexually aware than Stoker's modest
though compromised heroine: she is obviously attracted to the Count
during his daylight walks in London, and visits an early cinema
which is showing a semi-pornographic feature with 'Prince Vlad' in
Harker's absence. Finally, Van Helsing, in an aside that acknowledges
Daniel Farson's speculations regarding Stoker's sexual health in *The
Man Who Wrote Dracula*, also suggests that 'Civilization and syphi-
lization have advanced together'.[29]

Allusions to earlier *Dracula* films also abound within *Bram Stoker's
Dracula*: the title which is displayed following the prologue is accompanied by music reminiscent of the Hammer tradition; Harker's
coachman has long fingernails that recall both the 1922 *Nosferatu*
and the 1979 West-German remake *Nosferatu: Phantom der Nacht*,
directed by Werner Herzog; even one of the short black-and-white
films viewed by Mina and Prince Vlad suddenly switches into negative, in a manner that recalls Hutter's coach journey in Murnau's
Nosferatu. *Bram Stoker's Dracula* is truly a *bricolage*, a collection of
fragments brought into conjunction only through the mediating
theme of its alleged fidelity to Stoker's 1897 novel.

Bram Stoker's Dracula is, in this respect, not so much a representation of a Victorian novel as the expression of those things the twentieth century is inclined to associate with its historical predecessor:
emphatically, the tense conjunction of both fearful sexual repression
and lush erotic desire behind rigid social hierarchies and stiff, restrictive
dress fabrics. If Coppola is embedding a overwhelmingly twentieth-
century view of what it is to be Victorian into the film, then his other
departure from a simple reproduction of Stoker's plot would be the
prologue and epilogue with which he surrounds the familiar plot of
Dracula. Coppola's prologue suggests that the Count's induction into
vampirism comes not through his study at the satanic Scholomance
(345) but is a consequence of his rejection of the Christian faith.
Vlad Tepes, a defender of that faith, sees his wife Elisebeta refused
Christian burial because she has committed suicide following a false
report of his death. In a scene which recalls Murnau's *Nosferatu*, the

Count sees Harker's miniature portrait of Mina, who is the perfect visual image – and thus implicitly the reincarnation – of the dead Elisebeta. His campaign thus becomes a twofold strategy to drain the mortal energy of London and to possess himself of Harker's wife, and is signified by the film's seeming subtitle, the motto 'Love Never Dies', which is displayed prominently on the film's marketing material. The prologue anticipates the epilogue, which is a significant departure from Stoker's plot. Mina retreats with the stricken Count (who she calls 'my love') into the Castle, excluding her defenders and husband from interference with the vampire's dying moments. He asks her to 'Give me peace': she completes the insertion of Morris's knife through his body and then decapitates him. The killing becomes an act of love rather than revenge, though the position of Mina is left ambiguous thereafter – the more so as the final tableau with the redemptive Harker child is not included. In a sense, therefore, despite the promise of its title, this is not *Bram Stoker's Dracula* at all. Neither, though, is it unequivocally 'Francis Ford Coppola's *Dracula*'. It is, rather, 'the Twentieth Century's *Dracula*', a summation not merely of the plot of Stoker's film, but of its various interpretations through both academic criticism and film production.

THE LITERARY AFTERLIFE OF *DRACULA*

Stoker did not write a sequel to *Dracula*, though his 1909 novel *The Lady of the Shroud* marked his brief return to the vampire theme – albeit with ironic undertones. The novel, which ultimately becomes a fable about Balkan politics and technological innovation, is punctuated by allusions both to the Gothic and to the precedents set up in *Dracula*: to cite but one example, the hero of the novel tabulates in detail the behaviour of the heroine and her bodily characteristics against conventions that would be immediately recognizable to the reader of Stoker's 1897 novel.[30] The only other work by the author that can be explicitly associated with *Dracula* is the posthumously published short story 'Dracula's Guest' which may – or may not – have been envisaged as a prologue for the novel.[31] Critics and biographers are, however, sometimes excessive in their determination to find prefigurations of, or allusions to, the Count in Stoker's fictions before and after 1897.[32]

Because of this lack of a definitive sequel under the author's own hand, Stoker's *Dracula* is effectively contained as a narrative: Stoker's

Dracula can only be extended by interpretation, analysis or adaptation. Its plot can advance no further – at least in any authorized form. But if *Dracula* the novel is Stoker's, then Dracula the character has passed beyond his ownership. Just as cinema has recirculated the plot of Stoker's novel, making it effectively independent of the novel, so fiction, too, has extruded the central character, making the Count a component of fictions beyond Stoker's geographical and historical portrayal, and indeed predicating more than one biography for the evocative vampire.

Twentieth- and twenty-first-century fictions based upon the character of Count Dracula usually fall into one of two broad categories. First there is a significant body of work that adopts or adapts Stoker's vampire (and, on occasions, other characters from *Dracula*) into narratives that prefigure, parallel or post-date the events of the novel.[33] These may, at times, grant the Count a voice, thus effectively correcting the negative interpretation placed upon him by Stoker's mortal, outraged narrators. Second, there is a more substantial – and withal, often more subtle – range of fictions that pay effective homage to *Dracula* either by referencing the novel or its cinematic adaptations, or by making free – and sometimes ironic – use of the vampire conventions established by these. These two categories are bridged by a third form of *Dracula*-inflected fiction, in which Stoker himself makes an appearance either as a historical character or, on occasions, as a fictionalized vampire hunter or expert on occult matters.[34]

The Count, for example, makes a notable fictional appearance in Brian Stableford's *The Empire of Fear* (1988), a novel which depicts a world politically and socially dominated by vampires, and thus not at all reminiscent of Stoker's Victorian London. Opening in 1623, the novel concerns not merely human resistance to the dominant vampire culture which simultaneously enslaves mortals and drains their substance, but also contrasts the representation of the Western and Eastern un-dead. Stoker's Count is here unequivocally depicted as 'The Voivode Vlad the Fifth – whose scribes signed him Dragulya, and who was known to the world as Vlad Tepes, the Impaler.'[35] This seventeenth-century warrior, though, is emphatically not a stylish aristocrat in the Lugosi tradition (indeed, such a figure would be inconceivable under the historical logic of *The Empire of Fear*). Rather, he is violent and short-tempered, and is an indulger in the apparently eastern vice of sodomy. The Voivode's treatment of one mortal is somewhat telling in this respect:

when the minstrel had been first brought to Dragulya's court he had fully expected the Impaler to drive a pointed stick up his arse and stand him up in the courtyard to die – uncomfortably slowly – as his own weight dragged his guts downwards about the point. Instead, it had been something else entirely that the noble prince had stuck into his anus, and instead of being killed he had been made immortal.[36]

As in academic criticism, blood and semen are closely aligned in this fictionalization. The notion of infection from the east, a component of Stoker's anti-Semitism as well as of more general British fears of national and racial decline, is here given a renewed impetus by implicit association with AIDS – then a comparatively new and little-understood medical condition, associated in the public eye with homosexual promiscuity. Vampirism is a disease or a disorder, blood a dangerous as well as provocatively sexual substance. The mortal, on the one hand, becomes rhetorically the cautious and the hetero-sexual in culture, battling a source of infection and seeking to impose or offer safe and morally incongruous alternatives to those 'afflicted': abstinence or safe sex in the 1990s, 'coloured tablets' in Stableford's novel.[37] The difficulty is the attractiveness of the lifestyle, even to the heterosexual mortal, and thus the novel ultimately becomes a protracted attempt to desexualize vampirism, to take it way from an association with 'unorthodox sexual intercourse', to distribute it equally among both sexes, to celebrate its potential for liberating the human.[38] *The Empire of Fear* anticipates later novels that more directly relate the condition of vampirism to variant interpretations, favourable and demonized, of the homosexual lifestyle, though its message, if one there is, is so occluded as to be almost meaningless.

A more explicit association of the Count with AIDS (though not necessarily with homosexual sexuality) was made in Dan Simmons's *Children of the Night*, published four years after *The Empire of Fear* in 1992. Set in the post-Communist Romania of 1989, Simmons's narrative concerns not merely the plight of the country's AIDS orphans but the fate of one such child whose blood contains regener-ative qualities. This child is the unknowing heir to a vampire empire whose structure simultaneously recalls the communist regime of the past and the corrupt business networks which have replaced it. That empire is headed by a world-weary Dracula, hardly in control of his minions and reconciled to his own dissolution.[39] The topical political fable of *Children of the Night*, though, is tempered by the Count's recollections of a century that has seen him transformed into an icon in popular culture. He is particularly scathing regarding Stoker's work, and its later interpretations:

> *I have read Stoker. I read his silly novel when it was first published in 1897 and saw the first stage production in London. Thirty-three years later I watched that bumbling Hungarian ham his way through one of the most inept motion pictures I have ever had the misfortune to attend. Yes, I have read and seen Stoker's abominable, awkwardly written melodrama, that compendium of confusions which did nothing but blacken and trivialize the noble name of Dracula.* (original italics)[40]

Much of Dracula's interpolated 'Dreams of Blood and Iron' are concerned with the reassertion of the heroic myth of Vlad Tepes over the literary one popularized by Stoker and his successors. The climactic scenario, in which the vampire's ancient castle is destroyed by twentieth-century explosives laid under the command of the Count, frees him from both the literary myth and the overwhelming sense of depression that characterizes his recollections. In what is almost an inversion of the demonic figure of fiction, Simmons's Count contemplates migration to western Europe or Japan and dependence upon a 'haemoglobin substitute': in the post-communist world, it would appear, 'energy and business' may be a surrogate life-blood.[41] At the close of his novel, Simmons's Dracula would appear to be a slightly less malignant partner in the un-dead franchise established in Hammer's *The Satanic Rites of Dracula*.

In most twentieth- and twenty-first-century vampire fictions, how-ever, Count Dracula is not an explicitly acknowledged presence but rather functions as a paradigm against which other vampires must be judged. As Margaret L. Carter argues, Stoker's *Dracula* has become 'the definitive model for subsequent vampire fiction. Works that have been written since either consciously imitate or deliberately subvert the conventions established by Stoker'.[42] Those conventions are at times compromised by the variations introduced by cinema, though Carter's statement is essentially sound. Anne Rice's *Interview with the Vampire*, in both its novelistic (1976) and cinematic (1994) forms, is a case in point. On the one hand, Rice's vampires favour a visual iconography that links them to both Stoker's Count and Lugosi's cinematic interpretation: Louis de Pointe du Lac favours a 'finely tailored black coat' which he enshrouds within 'the long folds of the cape' he affects in *Interview with the Vampire*, just as his mentor Lestat, in the sequel *The Vampire Lestat* (1985), is perceived as 'the pale and deadly lord in the velvet cloak'.[43] This conservatism, though, is offset by a lack of respect for those things held as sacred in the occult and Christian theologies of Stoker's *Dracula*: vampires cannot dissolve into elemental mist, do not fear stakes through the heart, have no real relationship to any religious conception of damnation, and find crucifixes aesthetically pleasing. Surface has triumphed over substance: style is crucial, but so much else associated with the vampire in literature and folklore is apparently, in Louis' measured, even cultured, words, 'bull-shit'.[44]

Rice's vampires represent a significant departure from the Stoker-inflected past, and are possibly the most influential of twentieth-century literary models for later fiction. Rice's *The Vampire Chronicles* – a series of novels, beginning with *Interview with the Vampire* which chart the further adventures of Louis, Lestat and their associates – have in particular popularized a tradition in modern vampire fiction in which the vampire is the unmediated narrator. This has in turn given rise to the so-called sympathetic vampire – conventionally, a vampire whose suffering and loneliness ought to attract the sympathy of the reader, even in the face of the persecution which usually attends the un-dead. As in criticism, so fiction has come to perceive an aura of liberation and spontaneity in the vampiric condition, and a corresponding repressive ambiance in the persecution and orthodoxy applied by the mortal vampire hunter. Such revisionism has arguably led to the gradual association of the vampire with homosexuality, and the vampire hunter with an intolerant heterosexual consciousness.

Interview with the Vampire provides more than enough textual prompts towards an association of homosexual and un-dead lifestyles. The early relationship between Louis and Lestat, though devoid of genital sexuality, is scripted very much in the manner of a rite de passage between one sexual identity and another. Louis is uneasy with having to share a coffin with his seducer, and 'begged Lestat to let me stay in the closet' – this being the classic symbolic location for a homosexual unwilling or unable to voice his gay identity to the greater world.[45] Close vampire relationships throughout Rice's *Vampire Chronicles* appear to be predominantly same-sex, and cross-sexual alliances seem fated to end in dissolution: in *Interview with the Vampire*, Louis sees Claudia and Madeleine destroyed by sunlight in a manner that recalls *Nosferatu* and Hammer rather than Stoker; in *The Vampire Lestat*, Lestat converts his mother to vampirism only to see her desert him.[46] The literary vampire remains a lone hunter, seeking at-best temporary alliances with his own kind, feasting promiscuously in dangerous places, risking exposure and death should his overtures be detected by the unwilling. There are very few literary collectives of the vampire kind to equal, for example, that depicted in Joel Schumacher's 1987 film, *The Lost Boys*.

One of the few is that depicted in Poppy Z. Brite's *Lost Souls* (1992), a novel which freely associates vampiric and gay identities. Stoker is again a reference point for these fictional vampires, and indeed for the mortals who wish to enter the vampiric lifestyle as converts or neophytes. Jessy, a girl who aspires to become a vampire, reads *Dracula*, not as fiction but as a lifestyle guide. The scene in which she literally seduces her father in order to drink his blood is almost a parody of Lucy's sexualized attempt to bring Arthur close enough to yield to her advances (256): 'I need your blood, Daddy. I'm hungry. Your Jessy's hungry. Come to me.'[47] If Jessy's father is driven more by lust following a long period of sexual abstinence, other, sexually active individuals find themselves drawn to desire vampirism through a contemplation of commonly held signifiers of the un-dead condition.

Christian, a New Orleans vampire, 'still wore a cloak, long and black and lined with silk, whenever he went out. Old habits died hard, if they ever died at all.'[48] Working as a bartender, he is mocked by Goth teenagers who address him as 'Count Dracula', yet he is still able to seduce a young gay man, who, on feeling the sting of Christian's fangs, questions 'Are you a vampire?', before pleading

> Make me one too . . . Please? I want to be one. I want to walk at night with you and fall in love and drink blood. Kill me. Make me into a vampire too. Bite me. Take me with you.

Christian's manipulations simultaneously extract both blood and semen from the young man, his final orgasm coinciding with the climactic end of his mortal existence. Yet Christian, within the logic of *Lost Souls*, cannot make the boy into a vampire in the way that Stoker's Count may induct his victims into un-death. Vampires are born, not made, within Brite's novel, and Christian 'could not turn the boy into one of his kind any more than the boy could have bitten him and turned him human'.[49]

The threat of the literary vampire, in Brite's incarnation at least, is no longer that of infection but merely a matter of predation: he may eat, but he will not convert. All those who aspire to vampirism will thus never be satisfied, and their hunger for the desirable state of un-death, a desire which they are now empowered to confess by the relaxed morals of modern culture, will lead them as easy prey to the vampires. The very danger signs which conventionally warn the mortal to flee the presence of the un-dead – the pallor, the fangs, the sexual ambiguity – are now actively sought out by the willing, hungry victim. The warning has become an advertisement, revulsion has become desire, and *Dracula* has now become as much a milepost on the alluring trail towards un-death as it ever was an affirmation of the ultimate triumph of mortal morality. With the inversion of conventional morality in modern vampire fiction, the rise of the sympathetic vampire, and the rescheduling of the vampire hunter as representative of an undesirable moral and mortal state, the literary future would now appear to belong to the Count and his successors.

CHAPTER 6

GUIDE TO FURTHER READING

SCHOLARLY EDITIONS OF *DRACULA*

Stoker, Bram (2007), *Dracula*, ed. William Hughes and Diane Mason. Bath: Artswork Books. [Student edition which contains an introduction that surveys criticism from 1959 to 2007, a thematically ordered bibliography and a chronology of Stoker's life and writings.]

Stoker, Bram (2002), *Dracula*, ed. John Paul Riquelme. New York: Bedford/St Martin's. [Comparatively few notes but extensive appendices which include contemporary cartoons and sources as well as a selection of critical essays.]

Stoker, Bram (2000a), *Dracula*, ed. Glennis Byron. Peterborough: Broadview. [First published 1998, with a thorough Introduction, chronology and appendices which include 'Dracula's Guest' and extracts from contemporary reviews and other contexts.]

Stoker, Bram (1998), *Dracula Unearthed*, ed. Clive Leatherdale. Westcliff-on-Sea: Desert Island Books. [Hardback edition with around 3,500 annotations, not all of which are strictly necessary. Contains a useful checklist of Stoker's documented sources for *Dracula*.]

Stoker, Bram (1997a), *Dracula*, ed. Nina Auerbach and David J. Skal. New York: W. W. Norton. [Contains extracts from critical works, contemporary reviews and sources, as well as information on cinematic adaptation.]

Stoker, Bram (1993), *The Essential Dracula*, ed. Leonard Wolf. New York: Plume. [First published in 1975, an annotated and illustrated edition which includes the text of 'Dracula's Guest' and a table of film adaptations.]

Stoker, Bram (1983), *Dracula*, ed. A. N. Wilson. Oxford: Oxford University Press. [Sparsely annotated, and with an inaccurate chronology and minimal bibliography, this edition is distinguished only by its Introduction's grudging acceptance of Stoker's novel into the academic canon.]

OTHER WORKS BY STOKER

Stoker, Bram (2002), *A Glimpse of America and Other Lectures, Interviews and Essays*, ed. Richard Dalby. Westcliff-on-Sea: Desert island Books. [A useful compendium which also contains 'The Censorship of Fiction' and 'The American Tramp Question'.]

Stoker, Bram (2000b), *The Lady of the Shroud*, ed. William Hughes. Westcliff-on-Sea: Desert Island Books. [Annotated edition of Stoker's 1909 *faux* vampire narrative, set on the Balkan coast in the early twentieth century.]

Stoker, Bram (1999), *The Primrose Path*, ed. Richard Dalby. Westcliff-on-Sea: Desert Island Books. [Contains 'The Primrose Path' and 'Buried Treasures', two early serial works, first published in Ireland in 1875.]

Stoker, Bram (1997b), *Best Ghost and Horror Stories*, ed. Richard Dalby, Stefan Dziemianowicz and S. T. Joshi. New York: Dover. [Contains all the stories posthumously published in *Dracula's Guest*, with a number of early short stories including Stoker's first published work, 'The Crystal Cup'.]

Stoker, Bram (1990), *The Snake's Pass*. Dingle: Brandon. [Stoker's first novel, published in 1890. Set in Ireland and rich in dialect, it features a moneylender who is insultingly described as a vampire.]

Stoker, Bram (1973), *The Bram Stoker Bedside Companion*, ed. Charles Osborne. London: Victor Gollancz. [Contains the Scottish tale *The Watter's Mou'* as well as short stories from *Dracula's Guest*.]

Stoker, Bram (1906), *Personal Reminiscences of Henry Irving*. London: William Heinemann, 2 vols. [Also produced in a single volume edition in 1907, contains biographical details of Stoker's life in Ireland and descriptions of public figures which recall the Count's physiognomy.]

Stoker, Bram (1905), *The Man*. London: William Heinemann. [An anti-New Woman novel, anachronistically set in the Edwardian period. The undated paperback reprint by Wildside Press omits the anti-Semitic sentiments of the First Edition.]

BIOGRAPHIES AND BIBLIOGRAPHIES

Belford, Barbara (1996), *Bram Stoker: A Biography of the Author of Dracula*. London: Weidenfeld and Nicolson. [The first scholarly, illustrated biography of Stoker. Though at times fanciful and in places inaccurate, it is still a useful resource.]

Dalby, Richard and William Hughes (2004), *Bram Stoker: A Bibliography*. Westcliff-on-Sea: Desert Island Books. [Details first and later editions of all known writings by Stoker. Also features a comprehensive listing of reviews and criticism and a biography of Stoker.]

Farson, Daniel (1975), *The Man Who Wrote Dracula*. London: Michael Joseph. [Popular biography of Stoker by the author's great-nephew. Contains some quotable material from family documents, and is the source of the allegation that Stoker died of syphilis.]

Ludlam, Harry (1962), *A Biography of Dracula: The Life Story of Bram Stoker*. London: Foulsham Press. [The earliest biography of Stoker. Conversational rather than academic, this contains material from family documents and is especially strong on the author's theatrical career.]

Murray, Paul (2004), *From the Shadow of Dracula: A Life of Bram Stoker*. London: Jonathan Cape. [The best biography currently available. Thoroughly researched and balanced between literary and theatrical concerns, this contains previously unseen material from within the Stoker family.]

Osborough, Niall (1999), 'The Dublin Castle Career (1866–78) of Bram Stoker', *Gothic Studies*, 1/2, 222–40. [A thorough and detailed account of Stoker's legal career.]

Peter Haining and Peter Tremayne (1997), *The Un-Dead: The Legend of Bram Stoker and Dracula*. London: Constable. [A worthwhile resource which is especially strong on Stoker's early years in Ireland.]

GENERAL STUDIES AND EDITED COLLECTIONS

Byron, Glennis, ed. (1999), *Dracula: Contemporary Critical Essays*. Basingstoke: Macmillan. [Useful Casebook which presents extracts from many of the works mentioned in this *Reader's Guide*. Featured critics include David Punter, Phyllis Roth, Franco Moretti, Christopher Craft, Stephen Arata and Nina Auerbach.]

Gelder, Ken (1994), *Reading the Vampire*. London: Routledge. [*Dracula* is discussed on pp. 65–85, though the volume is an excellent resource for the study of literary vampires generally.]

Glover, David (1996), *Vampires, Mummies, and Liberals: Bram Stoker and the Politics of Popular Fiction*. Durham: Duke University Press. [Surveys the breadth of Stoker's fiction, with particular reference to Stoker's political philosophy.]

Hughes, William (2000), *Beyond Dracula: Bram Stoker's Fiction and Its Cultural Context*. Basingstoke: Macmillan. [Surveys the breadth of Stoker's fiction with particular reference to the contemporary debates on gender, faith and medicine.]

Hughes, William and Andrew Smith, eds (1998), *Bram Stoker: History, Psychoanalysis and the Gothic*. Basingstoke: Macmillan. [Twelve original essays on Stoker from a variety of theoretical perspectives.]

Leatherdale, Clive, ed. (1995), *The Origins of Dracula: The Background to Bram Stoker's Gothic Masterpiece*. Westcliff-on-Sea: Desert Island Books. [First published in 1987, this collection contains extracts from works mentioned in Stoker's manuscript notes to *Dracula*.]

Leatherdale, Clive (2001), *Dracula: The Novel and the Legend*, Third Edition. Westcliff-on-Sea: Desert Island Books. [First published in 1985, and extensively revised for this edition. A fair introduction to the themes, characters and criticism of *Dracula*.]

Menegaldo, Gilles and Dominique Sipière, eds (2005), *Dracula: Stoker/Coppola*. Paris: Ellipses. [Bilingual collection that includes Victor Sage's innovative reading of *Dracula* in the context of Victorian pornography.]

Miller, Elizabeth, ed. (2005), *Bram Stoker's Dracula: A Documentary Volume*. Detroit: Thomson Gale. [An essential reference work. Contains encyclopaedic coverage of Stoker's biography, research and writing practice as well as reviews, modern criticism and information on theatrical and cinematic adaptation.]

Senf, Carol (1998), *Dracula: Between Tradition and Modernism*. New York: Twayne. [A readable survey which covers contexts, narrative strategy, imperialism, religion, gender, social class and science.]

Shepard, Leslie and Albert Power, eds (1997), *Dracula: Celebrating 100 Years*. Dublin: Mentor Press. [Uneven in quality, this volume nonetheless presents valuable contributions not merely by Stoker critics but also through interviews with Bela Lugosi, Peter Cushing and Christopher Lee.]

Skal, David J. (1990), *Hollywood Gothic: The Tangled Web of Dracula from Novel to Stage to Screen*. New York: W. W. Norton.

[Basic information on the novel, but good coverage of pre-Hammer cinematic and stage adaptations.]

CRITICAL SPECIALISMS

Psychoanalysis

Bierman, Joseph (1972), '*Dracula*: prolonged childhood illness and the oral triad'. *American Imago*, 29, 186–98. [Influential article which reads *Dracula* as an expression of sibling rivalry.]

    Lapin, Daniel (1995), *The Vampire, Dracula and Incest*. San Francisco: Gargoyle Press. [In part a study of modern cases of sexual abuse, this book argues that Stoker and his siblings were themselves subject to similar atrocities.]

    Richardson, Maurice (1959), 'The Psychoanalysis of Ghost Stories'. *The Twentieth Century*, 166, 419–31. [The first sustained critical work on *Dracula* and other Gothic texts, this often polemical work draws on the Oedipus Complex, Freud's *Totem and Taboo* and Ernest Jones's *On the Nightmare*.]

    Roth, Phyllis (1977), 'Suddenly sexual women in Bram Stoker's *Dracula*'. *Literature and Psychology*, 27, 113–21. [Identifies the core fantasy of *Dracula* as pre-Oedipal rather than Oedipal.]

    Roth, Phyllis (1982), *Bram Stoker*. Boston: Twayne. [The first serious full-length study of Stoker's writings. Identifies recurrent plot devices and unconscious preoccupations across Stoker's writings.]

Gender and Sexuality

Bentley, C. F. (1972), 'The monster in the bedroom: sexual symbolism in Bram Stoker's *Dracula*'. *Literature and Psychology*, 22, 27–34. [Suggests that Stoker was not aware of the sexual symbolism of his novel.]

    Craft, Christopher (1984), '"Kiss me with those red lips": gender and inversion in Bram Stoker's *Dracula*'. *Representations*, 8, 107–33. [Important reading of sexual identity, with a particular focus on male relationships.]

    Ledger, Sally (1997), *The New Woman: Fiction and Feminism at the Fin de Siècle*. Manchester: Manchester University Press. [Detailed study of the New Woman in fiction and culture, which considers *Dracula* on pp. 100–6.]

Schaffer, Talia (1994), 'A Wilde desire took me': the homoerotic history of *Dracula*', *ELH*, 61, 381–425. [Suggests that Stoker was closeted gay man, and *Dracula* a response to the trials of Oscar Wilde.]

Stevenson, John Allen (1988), 'A vampire in the mirror: the sexuality of *Dracula*'. *PMLA*, 103, 139–49. [A frequently quoted standard work on the Victorian sexuality of *Dracula*, and a good counterpart to Bentley's analysis.]

Medical Criticism

Flood, David Hume (1989), 'Blood and transfusion in Bram Stoker's *Dracula*'. *University of Mississippi Studies in English*, 7, 180–92. [Credible reading of the blood exchanges in the novel.]

Fontana, Ernest (1984), 'Lombroso's Criminal Man and Stoker's *Dracula*', *Victorian Newsletter*, 66, 25–7. [Important early reading of *Dracula* through scientific criminology. A good counterpart to the works of Pick and Sage.]

Hartnell, Elaine Marie (1998), 'Thoughts too long and too intensely fixed on one object: fictional representations of brain fever', in Nickianne Moody and Julia Hallam, eds, *Medical Fictions*. Liverpool: MCCA, pp. 201–12. [Locates Harker's physical breakdown in the context of nineteenth-century mental pathology.]

Mason, Diane (2008), *The Secret Vice: Masturbation in Victorian Fiction and Medical Culture*. Manchester: Manchester University Press. [Reads female behaviour in both *Dracula* and Le Fanu's 'Carmilla' through Victorian writings on masturbation.]

Pick, Daniel (1988), 'Terrors of the night: *Dracula* and "degeneration" in the late nineteenth century'. *Critical Quarterly*, 30/4, 71–97. [A more detailed reading of degeneration than that forwarded earlier by Fontana.]

Sage, Victor (1988), *Horror Fiction in the Protestant Tradition*. Basingstoke: Macmillan. [Reads degeneration in the context of the Protestant tradition of evidence and testimony. The book also contains a pertinent study of the diary structure of *Dracula*.]

Racial, Nationalistic and Political Criticism

Arata, Stephen D. (1990), 'The Occidental tourist: *Dracula* and the anxiety of reverse colonization', *Victorian Studies*, 33, 621–45.

[An important reading of the novel as but one expression of British fears of national and imperial decline at the turn of the twentieth century.]

Davison, Carol Margaret (2004), *Anti-Semitism and British Gothic Literature* Basingstoke: Palgrave. [A significant extension of Jules Zanger's earlier reading of anti-Semitism in *Dracula*, contextualized through a study of British Gothic fiction from the eighteenth century.]

Eagleton, Terry (1995), *Heathcliff and the Great Hunger*. London: Verso. [Provocative, and at times almost polemical, reading of *Dracula* as a political fable about Irish landlordism.]

Gibson, Matthew (2006), *Dracula and the Eastern Question: British and French Vampire Narratives of the British and French Near East.* Basingstoke: Palgrave. [Meticulous reading of both *Dracula* and *The Lady of the Shroud* in the context of British public opinion and foreign policy.]

Moretti, Franco (1982), 'The dialectic of fear'. *New Left Review*, 136, 67–85. [Important Marxist reading of *Dracula* as a representative of monopoly capitalism; interprets the death of Morris as a symbolic dissipation of British fears of a transatlantic rival.]

Zanger, Jules (1991), 'A sympathetic vibration: *Dracula* and the Jews', *ELT*, 34, 33–43. [Persuasive reading of the physiognomy and practices of the vampire in the context of anti-Semitic history.]

NOTES

CHAPTER 1. CONTEXTS

1. Bram Stoker, 1906: Vol. 1, 31.
2. Barbara Belford, 1996: 14; Peter Haining and Peter Tremayne, 1997: 47; Daniel Lapin, 1995: 24.
3. Barbara Belford, 1986: 51; Harry Ludlam, 1962: 19; Clive Leatherdale, 1985: 58.
4. The Committee of the Dublin University Football Club, 1954: 50–2, 65; Daniel Farson, 1975: 18.
5. See: Niall Osborough, 1999: 222–40, *passim*.
6. 'The Chain of Destiny' is reprinted with Stoker's first fiction, 'The Crystal Cup' in Bram Stoker, 1997b; 'The Primrose Path' (1875) and 'Buried Treasures' (1875) are reprinted in Bram Stoker, 1999. Clive Leatherdale's note to the latter volume strains to link the two works to *Dracula*: see Bram Stoker, 1999: 13, 14.
7. Stoker to *Blackwood's*, 6 October 1874. National Library of Scotland MS 4325 f. 240.
8. Laurence Irving, 1989: 453.
9. Daniel Farson, 1975: 215–16.
10. Daniel Farson, 1975: 234.
11. Reproduced in Elizabeth Miller, 2005: 27.
12. Three obituaries are reprinted in Elizabeth Miller, 2005: 23–6.
13. Paul Murray, 2004: 20–1.
14. Bram Stoker, 1906: Vol. 1, 32.
15. See William Hughes, 2000: 55–7.
16. Richard Ellmann, 1987: 57–8.
17. Barbara Belford, 1996: 40.
18. Quoted in Peter Haining and Peter Tremayne, 1997: 28.
19. Maurice Richardson, 1959: 429; Talia Schaffer, 1994: 381–425, *passim*.
20. See *A Glimpse of America* (1886) and 'The American Tramp Question and its relation to the Old English Vagrancy Laws', reprinted in Bram Stoker, 2002: 15, 168–70.
21. See Ernest Fontana, 1984: 25–7.
22. See Jules Zanger, 1991: 33–43; Carol Davison, 2004: 122–3.
23. These Jewish characters include the moneylenders Mr Cavendish in *The Man* and Mr Mendoza in *The Watter's Mou'* (1894; reprinted in Bram Stoker, 1973), as well as the London clothes merchant, Joshua Sheeny

Cohen Benjamin, in 'Crooken Sands' (1894; reprinted in Bram Stoker, 1997b).

24. Carol Davison, 2004: 132–3. See Chapter 3, pp. 36–8.
25. See Nina Auerbach, 1981: 281–300.
26. See Stephen D. Arata, 1990: 621–45.
27. Harker's position within the group is equivocal: See William Hughes, 1997b: 135.
28. Bram Stoker, 2002: 30.
29. See Hall Caine's 1912 assessment of Stoker's life and writings, reprinted in Elizabeth Miller, 2005: 24–6; and William Hughes, 'Dracula and other novels': Reviewing Stoker's Fiction, 1882–1912', in Richard Dalby and William Hughes, 2004: 19–20. See also Chapter 4, pp. 83–92.

CHAPTER 2. LANGUAGE, STYLE AND FORM

1. Glennis Byron, 1999: 1.
2. See, for example, 'The Trail of the Vampire', St James's Gazette, 30 June 1897, p. 5; The Spectator, 31 July 1897, pp. 150–1, reprinted in Elizabeth Miller, 2005: 265–6.
3. The Daily Mail, 1 June 1897, p. 3, reprinted in Elizabeth Miller, 2005: 258–9.
4. For an excellent survey of the Gothic from Walpole to Postmodernity, see Andrew Smith, 2007.
5. Clare Simmons, 1998: 29–30.
6. Ellen Moers, 1977: 90–9.
7. Fred Botting, 1994: 183.
8. Christopher Craft, 1984: 109–10.
9. Victor Sage, 1988: 182.
10. Andrew Smith, 2007: 114.
11. See Glasgow Herald, 10 June 1897, p. 10; The Spectator, 31 July 1897, pp. 150–1; and The Bookman, 12 (August 1897), p. 129, reprinted in Elizabeth Miller, 2005: 263, 266–7.
12. Surprisingly, despite the tone set by Stoker's reviewers and the obvious structural and character parallels between the two books, comparatively little critical work has compared The Woman in White and Dracula. See Mark M. Hennelly, 1982: 15–31; William Hughes, 2007: 136–48.
13. 'The Trail of the Vampire', reprinted in Elizabeth Miller, 2005: 265.
14. Wilkie Collins, 1998: 5.
15. For a reading of Lucy's surname see Clive Leatherdale, 2001: 144–5.
16. See William Hughes, 2005: 123–38.
17. See Marie Mulvey-Roberts, 1998: 78–95.
18. William Hughes 2000: 151–7.
19. Victor Sage, 1988: 54.
20. Morris's proposal to Lucy recalls Mark 1, v. 7 and inaccurately cites Matthew 25, vv. 1–10, before alluding to wagon-driving in 'double harness' (99). The use of slang, foreign language and cockney dialect in the

period is considered in Raymond Chapman, 1994: 12–50; and Victorian
Biblical allusion is considered in Michael Wheeler, 1979.
21. See Franco Moretti, 1982: 76; Andrew Smith, 2003: 4.
22. Victor Sage, 1988: 52.
23. See, for example, Charles Dickens, 1999: 215, 356.
24. Ardel Thomas, 2002: 84–99.
25. See Mark Hennelly, 1982: 24–7.

CHAPTER 3. READING *DRACULA*

1. Compare, for example, Phyllis Roth, 1977, and Robert Mighall, 1999;
   Stephanie Demetrakopoulos, 1977 and Katie Harse, 1998; Elizabeth
   Miller, 2005: 296–356, *passim*.
2. Maurice Richardson, 1959: 427; other critics who make similar claims
   regarding the primacy of sexual interpretations of *Dracula* include
   Burton Hatlen, 1980, and Dennis Foster, 2002: 484–5.
3. Robert Mighall, 1988: 74, 62.
4. Maurice Richardson, 1959: 428; Peter Redgrove and Penelope Shuttle,
   1994: 252.
5. C. F. Bentley, 1972: 27.
6. David Hume Flood, 1989: 186; William Hughes, 2000: 141.
7. Christopher Craft, 1984: 107; Jennifer Wicke, 1992: 493.
8. Seymour Shuster, 1973: 259; Daniel Lapin, 1995: 24; Maurice Richardson,
   1959: 247; cf. Phyllis Roth, 1982: 114–15.
9. See, for example, Victor Sage, 1988: 179–86; William Hughes, 2000:
   167–74; Roger Luckhurst, 2002: 208–13.
10. Leonard Wolf, 1993: 403, n. 25.
11. Ernest Fontana, 1984: 25–6.
12. Ernest Fontana, 1984: 25; Daniel Pick, 1988: 79, 81; cf. David Glover,
    1996: 68.
13. Ernest Fontana, 1984: 25.
14. William Hughes, 2000: 151–7.
15. Stephen D. Arata, 1990: 630.
16. Stephen D. Arata, 1990: 623.
17. Stephen D. Arata, 1990: 630.
18. Stephen D. Arata, 1990: 630; Branka Arsić, 2001: 551.
19. Carol M. Davison, 2004: 123, 130–1, 132.
20. Carol M. Davison, 2004: 122–3.
21. Bram Stoker, 1990: 26.
22. Carol M. Davison, 2004: 134–5.
23. Stoker's dramatization of the novel was performed only once at the
    Lyceum, simply to establish his copyright. See Paul Murray, 2004: 207–8.
24. George du Maurier, 1998: 11, 92.
25. George du Maurier, 1998: 282, 11.
26. Carol M. Davison, 2004: 121, 133.
27. George du Maurier, 1998: 211, 265.

28. See Nicholas Daly, 1999: 37. More than one critic has suggested that the hasty disposal of the Count (418–19) is less convincing (and potentially less final) than the earlier ritual exorcism of Lucy Westenra (259–61). See, for example, Elizabeth Miller, 2000: 108–9.
29. The only substantial reading of Harker's Brain Fever in the context of Victorian medicine is Elaine Hartnell, 1998: 201–4, 209–10.
30. Exceptions include William Hughes, 2000: 160–1.
31. See, for example, Maggie Kilgour, 1995: 12, 18–19, 163–4; Max Fincher, 2007: 142.
32. Quoted in Peter Haining, 1987: 112–14. See also David J. Skal, 1990: 185. Critical acknowledgements of the incest motif within *Dracula* include C. F. Bentley, 1972: 29; Christopher Craft, 1984: 108; and Carol Senf, 1998: 50–1. A provocative alternative reading can be found in John Allen Stevenson, 1988: 143.
33. Daniel Lapin, 1995: 20.
34. Carol Senf, 1998: 51; Showalter, 1991: 180.
35. Daniel Lapin, 1995: 20; cf. Carol Fry, 1972: 21; Phyllis Roth, 1982: 118.
36. Christopher Craft, 1984: 109.
37. John Allen Stevenson, 1988: 145.
38. Gail B. Griffin, 1980: 464, 463.
39. John Allen Stevenson, 1988: 109; Victor Sage, 1988: 185, 186.
40. Talia Shaffer, 1994: 401.
41. Christopher Craft, 1984: 109–10.
42. Daniel Lapin, 1995: 24. Lamia, the subject of John Keats's narrative poem of 1819, was a sorceress serpent transformed into a beautiful young woman by Hermes.
43. Nina Auerbach, 1995: 84; Talia Shaffer, 1994: 398.
44. Talia Shaffer, 1994: 398.
45. Talia Shaffer, 1994: 391.
46. Talia Shaffer, 1994: 381. For examples of those mechanisms see Talia Shaffer, 1994: 392, 396.
47. Carol Senf, 1998: 50.
48. Compare here not merely Harker's encounter with the female vampires (79–80), but also his comments upon peasant dress (43) and the inn-keeper's wife in Bistritz (44).
49. In Coppola's 1992 film, Mina says to Van Helsing 'I know that Lucy harboured secret desires for you; she told me so. I, too, know what men desire', before embracing him passionately.
50. Daniel Farson, 1975: 214.
51. For an indication of Stoker's model of approved masculine behaviour see Bram Stoker, 2002: 19.
52. See Bram Stoker, 1905: 64, 185, 236; Bram Stoker, 2000b: 231–2, 306–7.
53. Margot Gayle Backus, 1999: 136–7.
54. Ken Gelder, 1994: 77.
55. Carol Fry, 1972: 21.
56. William Hughes, 2000: 140, 194 n. 8.
57. Elaine Showalter, 1991: 180.
58. Victor Sage, 1988: 56.

59. Victor Sage, 2005: 58.
60. Victor Sage, 2005: 64.
61. Victor Sage, 2005: 60.
62. Nina Auerbach, 1995: 80.
63. Nina Auerbach, 1995: 79.
64. Jean Stengers and Anne Van Neck, 2001: 111–12.
65. Elaine Showalter, 1991: 181.
66. Victor Sage, 1988: 57.
67. Sos Eltis, 2002: 456.
68. William Hughes, 2000: 166.
69. Victor Sage, 1988: 57.
70. For an overview of the many aspirations and activities associated with the New Woman, see Sally Ledger, 1997: 9–31. See also Carol Senf, 1988: 60–4, for a reading structured around Stoker's novel and biography.
71. Sally Ledger, 1997: 17–18.
72. Sally Ledger, 1997: 105.
73. Sally Ledger, 1997: 106. The term 'angel in the house' refers to the idealized wife and mother figure in Coventry Patmore's sequence of poems published under the same title between 1854 and 1861.
74. Critics who interpret this scene through oral sexuality include Jean-Jacques Lecercle, 2001: 71; Victor Sage, 1988: 180.
75. Michel Foucault, 1984: 147.
76. Clive Leatherdale explicitly identifies Mina's consumption of blood as an allusion to the Roman Catholic Mass: see Clive Leatherdale, 2001: 200. For a more polemical reading of the Christian symbolism of *Dracula* see Christopher Gist Raible, 1979.
77. For a review of Mesmer's career, technique and theories see Derek Forrest, 2000: 1–69.
78. Derek Forrest, 2000: 23–7.
79. Derek Forrest, 2000: 72.
80. Derek Forrest, 2000: 161–8, 190–2.
81. Derek Forrest, 2000: 223–5; William Hughes, 2000: 168–9.
82. Derek Forrest, 2000: 10, 20–1.
83. George Du Maurier, 1998: 49. Mesmer was one of the figures included in his *Famous Impostors* (1910).
84. Derek Forrest, 2000: 85.
85. Christopher Craft, 1984: 116.
86. Christopher Gist Raible, 1979: 103; Clive Leatherdale, 2001: 193.
87. Bram Stoker, 1906: Vol. 1, 32.
88. The abbreviations stand for the following degrees: Doctor of Medicine; Doctor of Philosophy; Doctor of Letters', the latter often being an honorary degree. Seward, also, is a 'medico-jurist' (288), a physician associated with the application of medical science within the legal system.
89. Franco Moretti, 1982: 76.
90. Bram Stoker, 2002: 30.
91. Andrew Smith, 2003: 20–4.
92. Clive Leatherdale, 2001: 125.

93. Victor Sage, 1988: 183.
94. Victor Sage regards this physical resemblance as an allusion to Cesare Lombroso's theory that genius is a form of degeneration. See Victor Sage, 1988: 181–3.

CHAPTER 4. CRITICAL RECEPTION
AND PUBLISHING HISTORY

1. Student paperback editions have used a variety of cover images: the Oxford World's Classics edition (1983), displays an image of the Hungarian actor Bela Lugosi in Tod Browning's film *Dracula* (1931); the Penguin (1993) and Norton (1997) editions use the same image of Henry Irving as Mephistopheles; the Broadview reprint (2000a) features a Victorian photograph which teasingly recalls the initial attack on Lucy; while the Bedford St Martin's edition (2002) shows a landscape painting. The Artswork edition (2007) reproduces the original 1897 cover in colour.
2. *Daily Telegraph*, 24 April 1912; reprinted in Elizabeth Miller, 2005: 24, 26.
3. *Detroit Free Press*, 18 November 1899; reprinted in Elizabeth Miller, 2005: 272.
4. *Observer*, 1 August 1897; reprinted in Elizabeth Miller, 2005: 266.
5. *Manchester Guardian*, 15 June 1897; reprinted in Elizabeth Miller, 2005: 263.
6. *Bookman*, August 1897; reprinted in Elizabeth Miller, 2005: 267.
7. Reprinted in Elizabeth Miller, 2005: 267.
8. *Daily Mail*, 1 June 1897; reprinted in Elizabeth Miller, 2005: 258.
9. Stoker is compared to Collins in the *Glasgow Herald*, 10 June 1897, and the *Bookman*, 1897; Le Fanu is cited in comparison by the *Spectator*, 31 July 1897 and the *St James's Gazette*, 30 June 1897. These reviews are reprinted in Elizabeth Miller, 2005: 263, 267, 266 and 265, respectively.
10. *Publishers' Circular*, 7 August 1897: 131.
11. Reprinted in Elizabeth Miller, 2005: 265. Intriguingly, the opinions expressed by contemporary authors are more favourable: see the letters from M. E. Braddon and Arthur Conan Doyle, reprinted in Elizabeth Miller, 2005: 264, 267.
12. *Spectator*, 31 July 1897; reprinted in Elizabeth Miller, 2005: 266.
13. *Athenaeum*, 26 June 1897; reprinted in Elizabeth Miller, 2005: 264–5.
14. Reprinted in Elizabeth Miller, 2005: 263.
15. Reprinted in Elizabeth Miller, 2005: 266.
16. *Pall Mall Gazette*, 1 June 1897; reprinted in Elizabeth Miller, 2005: 260.
17. *Times*, 23 August 1897; reprinted in Elizabeth Miller, 2005: 268.
18. Reprinted in Elizabeth Miller, 2005: 268.
19. Reprinted in Elizabeth Miller, 2005: 270.
20. Reprinted in Elizabeth Miller, 2005: 270.
21. *San Francisco Wave*, 9 December 1899; reprinted in Elizabeth Miller, 2005: 272.

22. Reprinted in Elizabeth Miller, 2005: 272, 273.
23. Reprinted in Elizabeth Miller, 2005: 273.
24. Barbara Belford, 1996: xiv.
25. Bram Stoker, 2002: 155, 161.
26. Bram Stoker, 2002: 160.
27. Richard Dalby and William Hughes, 2004: 88.
28. Richard Dalby and William Hughes, 2004: 90.
29. Richard Dalby and William Hughes, 2004: 89.
30. Richard Dalby and William Hughes, 2004: 90.
31. Richard Dalby and William Hughes, 2004: 102–11, *passim*.
32. Richard Dalby and William Hughes, 2004: 91, 92.
33. A. N. Wilson, intriguingly, was at the time a regular contributor to the *Spectator*, one of the less favourable reviewers of *Dracula* in 1897.
34. *Bookman*, 1912: 347. In direct contrast, Stoker's obituary in the London *Times* dismissed *Dracula* as being typical of 'a particularly florid [*sic*] and creepy kind of fiction': see Elizabeth Miller, 2005: 24. Miller misquotes the original obituary, which substitutes 'lurid' for 'florid'.
35. Maurice Richardson, 1959: 427.
36. Maurice Richardson, 1959: 427.
37. Maurice Richardson, 1959: 427.
38. Maurice Richardson, 1959: 428, 427, 428–9.
39. David Punter, 1980: 256–63; Phyllis Roth, 1982: *passim*.
40. Phyllis Roth, 1982: 115.
41. Phyllis Roth, 1982: 111.
42. Seymour Shuster, 1973: 259, 268.
43. Joseph Bierman, 1972: 193.
44. Daniel Lapin, 1995: 29–31.
45. Daniel Farson, 1975: 214.
46. Penelope Shuttle and Peter Redgrove, 1986: 252.
47. Daniel Farson, 1975: 214, 234, 212.
48. Daniel Farson, 1975: 234; cf. Barbara Belford, 1996: 320–1; Leslie Shepard, 1997: 179.
49. Paul Murray, 2004: 267–9.
50. David Glover, 1996: 76–8; William Hughes, 2000: 141–9; David Hume Flood, 1989: 184–7.
51. Clive Leatherdale, 1997; Roger Luckhurst, 2002: 208–13; Bridget M. Marshall, 2000; Jani Scandura, 1996; L. Ledwon, 1993.
52. Jasmine Y. Hall, 1996; Anne McGillivray, 2002.
53. W. J. McCormack, 1991: 845.
54. Terry Eagleton, 1995: 215.
55. Seamus Deane, 1998: 90.
56. David Glover, 1996: 28.
57. David Glover, 1996: 29.
58. Vesna Goldsworthy, 1998: 83
59. Vesna Goldsworthy, 1998: 77–85; Eleni Coundouriotis, 1999–2000; Matthew Gibson, 2006: 69–95; S. T. Gürçaglar, 2001.
60. Daniel Farson, 1975: 15.
61. William Hughes, 2000: 137–8.

62. Daniel Farson, 1975: 214.
63. Alan Johnson, 1984: 21.
64. Alan Johnson, 1984: 26.
65. Phyllis Roth, 1977: 115.
66. Christopher Craft, 1984: 120.
67. Christopher Craft, 1984: 120.
68. Talia Schaffer, 1994: 397.
69. Christopher Craft, 1984: 109.
70. Christopher Craft, 1984: 110.
71. Christopher Craft, 1984: 124.
72. Richard Dalby and William Hughes, 2004: 142–79. A previous bibliography, published in the year of *Dracula*'s centenary, listed only 215 critical works: see William Hughes, 1997a: 57–73.

CHAPTER 5. ADAPTATION, INTERPRETATION AND INFLUENCE

1. Paul Murray, 2004: 207–8. Richard Dalby notes that, for a conventional Lyceum matinee on 20 June 1894, 'Prices ranged from four people in the best private box (four guineas each) to the gallery at one shilling per seat': Richard Dalby and William Hughes, 2004: 9.
2. Paul Murray, 2004: 247–8; David Skal, 1990: 43.
3. David Skal, 1990: 44, 55; J. Gordon Melton, 1994: 437.
4. Jill Nelmes, 2007: 69; David Skal, 1990: 48.
5. David Skal, 1990: 48.
6. 'Schreck', intriguingly, means 'fear', 'shock, or 'alarm' in German. This is a coincidence rather than a publicity stunt, however: Max Schreck *was* the actor's real name, and indeed was the name he had acted under in earlier film productions.
7. David Skal, 1990: 51.
8. David Skal, 1990: 60, 70.
9. Harry Ludlam, 1962: 152, 154; David Skal, 1990: 67–9.
10. Harry Ludlam, 1962: 154–5.
11. David Skal, 1990: 70.
12. Harry Ludlam, 1962: 155–61.
13. David Skal, 1990: 77, 79, 83–4.
14. David Skal, 1990: 85–6.
15. An advertising campaign had previously fixed the opening night as Friday 13 February, a date allegedly vetoed by director Tod Browning for superstitious reasons: see David Skal, 1990: 140–2. Among the contenders for the role of Count Dracula was Conrad Veidt, a German-born actor who played the role of Major Strasser in the 1942 film, *Casablanca*.
16. Daniel Farson, 1975: 214.
17. Clive Leatherdale, 2001: 144–5.
18. Jeffrey N. McMahan, 1991: 141; Poppy Z. Brite, 1992: 39.

19. David Skal, 1990: 188–9. Lugosi's funerary garb forms the basis of 'Bela's Plot' by Caitlín R. Kiernan, of the short stories in Poppy Z. Brite's 1997 vampire collection, *Love in Vein II*.
20. J. Gordon Melton, 1994: 48–9.
21. Harry Ludlam, 1962: 156–69.
22. Leslie Shepard and Albert Power, 1997: 131.
23. Matthew Bunson, 1993: 124.
24. Leslie Shepard and Albert Power, 1997: 131.
25. Cinematic adaptations included *Count Dracula* (1970), with Christopher Lee and Klaus Kinski; *Andy Warhol's Dracula* (1973); the Universal *Dracula* (1979), with Frank Langella; and *Nosferatu: Phantom der Nacht* (1979) with Klaus Kinski. Television adaptations included the 1970 BBC TV *Dracula* with Denholm Elliot; *Dracula* (1970), with Jack Palance; and the BBC TV *Count Dracula* (1978), with Louis Jourdan.
26. Leslie Shepard and Albert Power, 1997: 133.
27. Anne Rice, 1977: 23.
28. For an interpretation of the exchange of confidences between the two see Diane Mason, 2008: 38.
29. Daniel Farson, 1975: 233–5.
30. Bram Stoker, 2001: 121–2.
31. See Clive Leatherdale's excellent analysis of the relationship between the two works in Clive Leatherdale, 2001: 120–3. See also Elizabeth Miller, 2005: 228.
32. See, for example, Barbara Belford, 1996: 178; Clive Leatherdale, 2001: 81.
33. See, for example, Freda Warrington, 1997 – 'The chilling sequel to Bram Stoker's *Dracula*' – which chronicles the return of the Van Helsing circle to Transylvania, seven years' after the close of Stoker's novel.
34. For example, Mark Frost, 1994.
35. Brian Stableford, 1990: 368.
36. Brian Stableford, 1990: 369.
37. Brian Stableford, 1990: 514.
38. Brian Stableford, 1990: 477.
39. Dan Simmons, 1992: 157.
40. Dan Simmons, 1992: 297. Compare here the opinion of the lesbian vampire in Katherine V. Forrest, 1993: 215, who depicts Stoker as 'A historian' of vampirism, albeit 'a most limited one'.
41. Dan Simmons, 1992: 406.
42. Margaret L. Carter, 1997: 175.
43. Anne Rice, 1977: 6; Anne Rice, 1990: 507.
44. Anne Rice, 1977: 27.
45. Anne Rice, 1977: 45.
46. Anne Rice, 1977: 328 ; Anne Rice, 1990: 384–8.
47. Poppy Z. Brite, 1994: 79.
48. Poppy Z. Brite, 1994: 62.
49. Poppy Z. Brite, 1994: 211, 67.

BIBLIOGRAPHY

FICTION

Brite, Poppy Z. (1994), *Lost Souls*. London: Penguin. [First published 1992.]
Collins, Wilkie (1998), *The Woman in White*. Oxford: Oxford University Press. [First published 1860.]
Dalby, Richard (ed.) (1989), *Dracula's Brood: Neglected Vampire Classics*. Wellingborough: Equation.
Dickens, Charles (1999), *Oliver Twist*. Oxford: Oxford World's Classics. [First published 1837.]
du Maurier, George (1998), *Trilby*. Oxford: Oxford World's Classics. [First published 1894.]
Forrest, Katherine V. (1993), 'O Captain, My Captain', in Pam Keesey (ed.), *Daughters of Darkness: Lesbian Vampire Stories*. Pittsburgh: Cleis Press. [First published 1987.]
Frost, Mark (1994), *The List of Seven*. London: Arrow. [First published 1993.]
Kiernan, Caitlín R. (1998), 'Bela's Plot', in Poppy Z. Brite (ed.), *Love in Vein II*. New York: HarperPrism. [First published 1997.]
Kipling, Rudyard (2005), 'The Mark of the Beast', in Roger Luckhurst (ed.), *Late Victorian Gothic Tales*. Oxford: Oxford World's Classics. [First published 1891.]
McMahan, Jeffrey N. (1991), *Vampires Anonymous*. Boston: Alyson Publications.
Marsh, Richard (2004), *The Beetle*, Julian Wolfreys (ed.). Peterborough: Broadview. [First published 1897.]
Rice, Anne (1977), *Interview with the Vampire*. London: Futura. [First published 1976.]
Rice, Anne (1990), *The Vampire Lestat*. London: Futura. [First published 1985.]
Simmons, Dan (1992), *Children of the Night*. London: Headline.
Stableford, Brian (1990), *The Empire of Fear*. London: Pan. [First published 1988.]
Warrington, Freda (1997), *Dracula the Undead*. London: Penguin.
Wilde, Oscar (2006), *The Picture of Dorian Gray*. Oxford: Oxford World's Classics. [First published 1890.]

BIBLIOGRAPHY

CRITICISM

Auerbach, Nina (1981), 'Magi and maidens: the romance of the Victorian Freud', *Critical Inquiry*, 8, 281–300.

Auerbach, Nina (1995), *Our Vampires, Ourselves*. Chicago: University of Chicago Press.

Backus, Margot Gayle (1999), *The Gothic Family Romance: Heterosexuality, Child Sacrifice and the Anglo-Irish Colonial Order*. Durham: Duke University Press.

Botting, Fred (1994), '*Dracula*, romance and the Radcliffean Gothic', *Women's Writing*, 1/2, 181–201.

Bunson, Matthew (1993), *Vampire: The Encyclopaedia*. London: Thames and Hudson.

Carlson, M. M. (1977), 'What Stoker saw: the history of the literary vampire', *Folklore Forum*, 10, 26–32.

Carter, Margaret L. (1997), 'Share alike: *Dracula* and the sympathetic vampire in mid-twentieth century pulp fiction', in Carol M. Davison (ed.), *Bram Stoker's Dracula: Sucking through the Century*. Toronto: Dundurn Press. pp. 175–94.

Chapman, Raymond (1994), *Forms of Speech in Victorian Fiction*. Harlow: Longman.

Committee of the Dublin University Football Club, The (1954), *Dublin University Football Club 1854–1954*. Dublin: Mountford.

Coundouriotis, Eleni (1999–2000), '*Dracula* and the idea of Europe', *Connotations*, 9/2, 143–59.

Dalby, Richard (1983), *Bram Stoker: A Bibliography of First Editions*. London: Dracula Press.

Daly, Nicholas (1999), *Modernism, Romance and the Fin de Siècle*. Cambridge: Cambridge University Press.

Deane, Seamus (1998), *Strange Country*. Oxford: Clarendon Press.

Demetrakopoulos, Stephanie (1977), 'Feminism, sex role exchanges, and other subliminal fantasies in Bram Stoker's *Dracula*', *Frontiers: A Journal of Women's Studies*, 2, 104–13.

Denman, Peter (1974), 'Le Fanu and Stoker: a probable connection', *Éire-Ireland*, 9, 152–8.

Ellmann, Richard (1987), *Oscar Wilde*. London: Hamish Hamilton.

Eltis, Sos (2002), 'Corruption of the blood and degeneration of the race: *Dracula* and policing the borders of gender', in Bram Stoker, *Dracula*, ed. John Paul Riquelme. New York: Bedford/St Martin's. pp. 450–65.

Fincher, Max (2007), *Queering Gothic in the Romantic Age: The Penetrating Eye*. Basingstoke: Palgrave.

Forrest, Derek (2000), *Hypnotism: A History*. London: Penguin. [First published 1999.]

Foster, Dennis (2002), '"The little children can be bitten": a hunger for Dracula', in Bram Stoker, *Dracula*, ed. John Paul Riquelme. New York: Bedford/St Martin's. pp. 483–99.

Foucault, Michel (1984), *The History of Sexuality: An Introduction*, Robert Hurley, (trans.). London: Penguin. [First published in 1976 in French, translated 1978.]

Fry, Carol (1972), 'Fictional conventions and sexuality in *Dracula*', *Victorian Newsletter*, 42, 20–2.

Garnett, Rhys (1990), '*Dracula* and *The Beetle*: imperial and sexual guilt and fear in late Victorian fantasy', in Rhys Garnett and R. J. Ellis (eds), *Science Fiction Roots and Branches: Contemporary Critical Approaches*. New York: St Martin's Press. pp. 30–54.

Goldsworthy, Vesna (1998), *Inventing Ruritania: The Imperialism of the Imagination*. New Haven: Yale University Press.

Griffin, Gail B. (1980), '"Your girls that you all love are mine": *Dracula* and the Victorian male sexual imagination', *International Journal of Women's Studies*, 3, 454–65.

Gürçaglar, S. T. (2001), 'Adding towards a nationalist text: on a Turkish translation of *Dracula*', *Target*, 13/1, 125–48.

Hall, Jasmine Y. (1996), 'Solicitors soliciting: the dangerous circulations of professionalism in *Dracula* (1897)', in Barbara Leah Harman and Susan Meyer (eds), *The New Nineteenth Century: Feminist Readings of Underread Victorian Fiction*. New York: Garland. pp. 99–116.

Harse, Katie (1998), '"Stalwart manhood": failed masculinity in *Dracula*', in Elizabeth Miller, (ed.), *Dracula: The Shade and the Shadow*. Westcliff-on-Sea: Desert Island Books. pp. 229–38.

Hatlen, Burton (1980), 'The return of the repressed/oppressed in Bram Stoker's *Dracula*', *Minnesota Review*, 15, 80–97.

Hennelly, Mark M. (1982), 'Twice-told tales of two counts: *The Woman in White* and *Dracula*', *The Wilkie Collins Society Journal*, 2, 15–31.

Hughes, William (1997a), *Bram Stoker (1847–1912): A Bibliography*. Brisbane: Victorian Fiction Research Unit.

Hughes, William (1997b), '"For the Blood is the Life": The construction of purity in Bram Stoker's *Dracula*', in Tracey Hill (ed.), *Decadence and Danger: Writing, History and the Fin de Siècle*. Bath: Sulis Press. pp. 128–37.

Hughes, William (2004), '*Dracula* and other novels': reviewing Stoker's fiction, 1882–1912', in Richard Dalby and William Hughes, *Bram Stoker: A Bibliography*. Westcliff-on-Sea: Desert Island Books. pp. 13–31.

Hughes, William (2005), 'Delusions of pallor: sanguine depletion, eroticism and the economics of blood in *Dracula*', in Claude Fierobe (ed.), *Dracula: Mythe et Métamorphoses*. Villeneuve d'Asq: Presses Universitaires du Septentrion. pp. 123–38.

Hughes, William (2007), 'Habituation and incarceration: asylum abuse in *The Woman in White* and *Dracula*', in Andrew Mangham (ed.), *Wilkie Collins; Interdisciplinary Essays*. Newcastle: Cambridge Scholars Publishing. pp. 136–48.

Kilgour, Maggie (1995), *The Rise of the Gothic Novel*. London: Routledge.

Irving, Laurence (1989), *Henry Irving: The Actor and His World*. London: Columbus Books.

Johnson, Alan (1984), '"Dual life": the status of women in Stoker's *Dracula*'. *Tennessee Studies in Literature*, 27, 20–39.

Leatherdale, Clive (1985), *Dracula: The Novel and the Legend*. Wellingborough: Aquarian Press.

Lecercle, Jean-Jacques (2001), 'The kitten's nose: *Dracula* and witchcraft', in Fred Botting (ed.), *The Gothic: Essays and Studies*. Cambridge: D. S. Brewer. pp. 71–86.

Ledwon, L. (1993), '*Dracula* and the Contagious Diseases Acts: the limits of the visible and the spectacle of prostitution', *Semiotics and the Human Sciences*, 7, 181–202.

Luckhurst, Roger (2002), *The Invention of Telepathy, 1870–1901*. Oxford: Oxford University Press.

McCormack, W. J. (1991), 'Irish Gothic and after (1820–1945)', in Seamus Deane (ed.), *The Field Day Anthology of Irish Writing*, Vol. 2. Londonderry: Field Day Publications. pp. 831–54.

McGillivray, Anne (2002), '"What sort of grim adventure was it on which I had embarked?": lawyers, vampires and the melancholy of law', *Gothic Studies*, 4/2, 116–32.

Marshall, Bridget M. (2000), 'The face of evil: phrenology, physiognomy and the Gothic villain', *Hungarian Journal of English and American Studies*, 6, 161–72.

Melton, J. Gordon (1994), *The Vampire Book*. Detroit: Visible Ink Press.

Mighall, Robert (1999), *A Geography of Victorian Gothic Fiction: Mapping History's Nightmares*. Oxford: Oxford University Press.

Miller, Elizabeth (2000), *Dracula: Sense and Nonsense*. Westcliff-on-Sea: Desert Island Books.

Moers, Ellen (1977), *Literary Women*. London: W. H. Allen.

Mulvey-Roberts, Marie (1998), '*Dracula* and the doctors: bad blood, menstrual taboo and the New Woman', in William Hughes and Andrew Smith (eds), *Bram Stoker: History, Psychoanalysis and the Gothic*. Basingstoke: Macmillan. pp. 78–95.

Nelmes, Jill (2007), *Introduction to Film Studies*, Fourth Edition. London: Routledge.

Punter, David (1980), *The Literature of Terror: A History of Gothic Fictions from 1765 to the Present Day*. London: Longman.

Raible, Christopher Gist (1979), 'Dracula: Christian heretic', *Christian Century*, 96, 103–4.

Redgrove, Peter, and Penelope Shuttle (1994), *The Wise Wound: Menstruation and Everywoman*. London: HarperCollins. [First published in 1978.]

Sage, Victor (2005), '*Dracula* and the codes of Victorian pornography', in Menegaldo, Gilles and Dominique Sipière (eds), *Dracula: Stoker/Coppola*. Paris: Ellipses. pp. 55–69. [First published in 1996.]

Scandura, Jani (1996), 'Deadly professions: *Dracula*, undertakers and the embalmed corpse', *Victorian Studies*, 40/1, 1–31.

Seed, David (1985), 'The narrative method of *Dracula*', *Nineteenth Century Fiction*, 40, 61–75.

Showalter, Elaine (1991), *Sexual Anarchy: Gender and Culture at the Fin de Siècle*. London: Bloomsbury. [First published in 1990.]

Shuster, Seymour (1973), '*Dracula* and surgically induced trauma in children', *British Journal of Medical Psychology*, 46, 259–70.

Simmons, Clare (1998), 'Fables of continuity: Bram Stoker and medieval-ism', in William Hughes and Andrew Smith (eds), *Bram Stoker: History, Psychoanalysis and the Gothic*. Basingstoke: Macmillan. pp. 29–46.

Smith, Andrew (2003), 'Demonising the Americans: Bram Stoker's postco-lonial Gothic', *Gothic Studies*, 5/2, 20–31.

Smith, Andrew (2007), *Gothic Literature*. Edinburgh: Edinburgh University Press.

Stengers, Jean, and Anne Van Neck (2001), *Masturbation: The History of a Great Terror*, Kathryn Hoffmann (trans.). Basingstoke: Palgrave.

Thomas, Ardel (2002), 'Thieves at the dinner table: queer, racial and national amalgamations in Wilkie Collins' *The Moonstone*', in Andrew Smith, Diane Mason and William Hughes (eds), *Fictions of Unease: The Gothic from Otranto to The X-Files*. Bath: Sulis Press. pp. 84–99.

Wheeler, Michael (1979), *The Art of Allusion in Victorian Fiction*. Basing-stoke: Macmillan.

Wicke, Jennifer (1992), 'Vampiric typewriting: *Dracula* and its media', *ELH*, 59, 467–93.

Winthrop-Young, Geoffrey (1994), 'Undead networks: information pro-cessing and media boundary conflicts in *Dracula*', in Donald Bruce and Anthony Purdy (eds), *Literature and Science*. Amsterdam: Rodopi. pp. 107–29.

INDEX